T0328961

CAMBRIDGE LIBRARY COLLECTION

Books of enduring scholarly value

British and Irish History, Nineteenth Century

This series comprises contemporary or near-contemporary accounts of the political, economic and social history of the British Isles during the nineteenth century. It includes material on international diplomacy and trade, labour relations and the women's movement, developments in education and social welfare, religious emancipation, the justice system, and special events including the Great Exhibition of 1851.

Landlords and Allotments

The agrarian interests of politician William Hillier Onslow (1853–1911), fourth earl of Onslow, led to his briefly becoming a cabinet minister as president of the Board of Agriculture and Fisheries in 1903–5, but he became convinced that the government of the day took no real interest in farming and food – to the extent that in 1914, sixty per cent of British food was imported. He had already decided that English landowners should, at a time of agricultural depression, help the labourers on their estates by making allotments of land available to them, and he published this work in 1886, in the hope of achieving a voluntary extension of the allotment system. It provides a historical context, examines in detail the current situation, and discusses the pros and cons of voluntary versus compulsory ceding of land, while providing insights into the development of the allotment movement.

Cambridge University Press has long been a pioneer in the reissuing of out-of-print titles from its own backlist, producing digital reprints of books that are still sought after by scholars and students but could not be reprinted economically using traditional technology. The Cambridge Library Collection extends this activity to a wider range of books which are still of importance to researchers and professionals, either for the source material they contain, or as landmarks in the history of their academic discipline.

Drawing from the world-renowned collections in the Cambridge University Library and other partner libraries, and guided by the advice of experts in each subject area, Cambridge University Press is using state-of-the-art scanning machines in its own Printing House to capture the content of each book selected for inclusion. The files are processed to give a consistently clear, crisp image, and the books finished to the high quality standard for which the Press is recognised around the world. The latest print-on-demand technology ensures that the books will remain available indefinitely, and that orders for single or multiple copies can quickly be supplied.

The Cambridge Library Collection brings back to life books of enduring scholarly value (including out-of-copyright works originally issued by other publishers) across a wide range of disciplines in the humanities and social sciences and in science and technology.

Landlords
and Allotments

The History and
Present Condition of the Allotment System

WILLIAM HILLER

CAMBRIDGE
UNIVERSITY PRESS

CAMBRIDGE
UNIVERSITY PRESS

University Printing House, Cambridge, CB2 8BS, United Kingdom

Cambridge University Press is part of the University of Cambridge.
It furthers the University's mission by disseminating knowledge in the pursuit of
education, learning and research at the highest international levels of excellence.

www.cambridge.org
Information on this title: www.cambridge.org/9781108080125

© in this compilation Cambridge University Press 2015

This edition first published 1886
This digitally printed version 2015

ISBN 978-1-108-08012-5 Paperback

LANDLORDS AND ALLOTMENTS

THE HISTORY AND PRESENT CONDITION

OF THE ALLOTMENT SYSTEM

BY THE

EARL OF ONSLOW

HONORARY SECRETARY OF THE LAND AND GLEBE OWNERS' ASSOCIATION
FOR THE VOLUNTARY EXTENSION OF THE ALLOTMENTS SYSTEM

LONDON

LONGMANS, GREEN, AND CO.

1886

PRINTED BY
SPOTTISWOODE AND CO., NEW-STREET SQUARE
LONDON

PREFACE.

IN endeavouring to arrive at a right judgment as to the duties and alleged shortcomings of proprietors in the provision of Allotments for the labourers employed on the estates of the large landowners, I was struck by the difficulty of obtaining any trustworthy statistics, with the exception of those published thirteen years ago, accompanying the Agricultural returns for 1873.

I therefore made it my business to endeavour to supply the want by making inquiries direct from my fellow-landowners. From the fact of these returns being collected chiefly from friends only, they are necessarily incomplete and imperfect; yet as far as they go are accurate, and will, I think, be interesting to the public as bearing upon a subject now prominently before Parliament, and upon which much misconception exists.

The result arrived at from a careful consideration of the facts here placed before the reader is that on every well-managed estate allotments exist, at rents

only higher than adjoining farm land by reason of the
outgoings having to be borne by the landowner, or
because, if devoted to other than agricultural purposes,
they would command a high rent. It is also made
evident that landowners, far from desiring to alienate
the labourer from the soil, have for many years past
and are still from day to day endeavouring to increase
the interest which he has in the cultivation of the
land upon which he lives.

It may be said that the landowners of England
have land available, which they are willing of their
own accord to devote to allotments, amply sufficient
to supply every labourer who desires it with such an
amount as he can cultivate during the hours which he
can spare from his regular employment.

I have collected from existing publications many
facts which, though not new to country folk, will contain
some information to dwellers in cities, and have never
before been dealt with collectively. I have taken the
liberty of making copious extracts from the writings of
Sir Edward Colebrook, Sir John Lawes, the Earl of
Tankerville, Colonel Edwards, Lord Tollemache, Mr.
Fredk. Impey, Sir Thos. Dyke Acland, Dr. Gilbert, and
The Small Farms and Labourers' Land Association, to
all of whom I wish to convey my sincere thanks.

ONSLOW.

THE LAND AND GLEBE OWNERS' ASSOCIATION FOR THE VOLUNTARY EXTENSION OF THE ALLOTMENTS SYSTEM.

Temporary Office: 7 Richmond Terrace, Whitehall, London, S.W.

President: HIS GRACE THE DUKE OF WESTMINSTER, K.G.

Vice-Presidents:

HIS GRACE THE DUKE OF BEAUFORT, K.G.
HIS GRACE THE DUKE OF MANCHESTER.
THE EARL OF PEMBROKE.
THE EARL STANHOPE.
THE EARL OF EGMONT.
THE EARL NELSON.
LORD SUFFIELD.

LORD HENLEY.
LORD WENLOCK.
LORD ALINGTON.
LORD TOLLEMACHE OF HELM-INGHAM.
LORD MOUNT-TEMPLE.
HON. M. FINCH-HATTON, M.P.
SIR W. BARTTELOT, M.P.
WALTER LONG, ESQ., M.P.

Hon. Secretary: THE EARL OF ONSLOW.

THIS Association has been formed for the purpose of extending the practice already prevalent on many estates of letting small quantities of land in allotments, inclusive of cottage gardens, either of pasture for the keep of a cow or of arable for cultivation.

The evidence given before the Royal Commission on the Housing of the Working Classes shows that any material rise in the wages of the labourer is not likely to take place so long as the present agricultural depression continues; the question therefore which remains to be solved is, how can the pecuniary condition of the agricultural labourer be improved, without diverting for his benefit the property of any other class of the community? The only capital of the agricultural labourer is his labour, and the way in which he can best be benefited is by increasing the return upon this capital. It is admitted on all hands that the poor man who has an allotment ungrudgingly bestows labour upon it before and after his regular hours of work, and that the result of this additional labour, both on his own and his family's part, is shown by a material improvement in his social as well as financial position. The farmers do not complain that the labour bestowed on small allotments is to the detriment of that for which they pay wages.

It has been found that the rents of allotments are paid punctually, that the labourer is able to bestow on the land manure amply sufficient to maintain its fertility, and that a class of small tenantry is created, grateful for the opportunities afforded and willing to pay a fair value for the land. The opportunity now occurs for landowners to show that there exists no necessity for any compulsory legislation on this subject, and that the objects which it has been proposed to attain by laws of very doubtful advantage to the classes not connected with the soil can be, and are being, accomplished by the voluntary action of the only persons who have the power, namely, the landowners.

Some statements made during the recent General Election have led a portion of the public to believe that there is a disinclination on the part of landowners to let land in allotments, but this is by no means the fact ; the system has been in operation for more than 100 years, and statistics in the possession of the Association show that it has been adopted to a greater or less extent by landowners possessing upwards of 1,500,000 acres of land in England and Wales. A very large majority of these noblemen and gentlemen have expressed their willingness to devote a further portion of their estates to this purpose, wherever tenants can be found.

The clergy who are owners of glebe lands, especially where the glebe lies close to a village, can also largely assist in the work. Those who are willing to promote the objects of the Association in their own districts are specially requested to send in their names to the Honorary Secretary.

The Association have a mass of information from landowners in all parts of the country as to the operation of the system. They are prepared to supply Forms of Agreement, which have been tested by long experience and found to work well. The Allotments Act, 1882, requires that trustees of lands left for the benefit of the poor should offer that land to agricultural labourers in allotments. Many such bodies of trustees are ignorant of the provisions of the Act, and it is one of the objects of this Association to bring it to their notice.

OBJECTS OF THE ASSOCIATION.

1. To obtain and disseminate information respecting the letting of land in allotments ; the formation and management of Cow Clubs ; the temporary letting of land for potato ground, or other plans for giving to artisans and labourers an interest in the cultivation of the soil.

2. To ascertain and make public the extent to which the system has already been applied, and how far the demand for further extension exists.

3. To urge upon landowners and employers of labour the desirability, in the interests of all three classes connected with the cultivation of the soil, of extending the system till every resident agricultural labourer of good character has, should he desire it, an allotment of land.

4. To call the attention of trustees of charity lands to the provisions of the Allotments Act, 1882.

Although the Association is in no sense a political one, it will be one of its objects to contradict misstatements of facts on the subject of allotments, and to explain to the labourers that the voluntary action of landowners is more likely to obtain for them speedily, on just conditions and at fair rents, garden and field allotments, than the operation of local bodies bound to respect the interests of the ratepayers, and exercising their powers compulsorily and in antagonism to the owners of land.

The Association hope to receive the liberal support of all land and glebe owners, as well as of the moderate men of both parties, in carrying out a work which has been conclusively shown to benefit all those interested, and which, if extended to its full limits, will attach the whole body of agricultural labourers, who now have so large a share in the direction of the destinies of the empire, to the land of this kingdom, without interfering with the rights of any other class.

LANDLORDS AND ALLOTMENTS.

INTRODUCTION.

PERHAPS the most striking feature of the recent electoral campaign, and that which distinguishes it most from its predecessors, is the ready manner in which politicians of both parties ascribed the utterance of falsehood to their opponents. For example, Lord Salisbury, speaking of the attacks of the Liberal party on the action of the Conservatives towards the Franchise Bill, said : 'The cry has been, "*Magnum est mendacium et prævalebit*"; they believe in the unlimited power of misrepresentation and falsehood.'

Mr. Chamberlain, at the meeting of the Allotments and Small Holdings Association, said: 'The Tories have lied on this subject with a vigour and a pertinacity and a unanimity which had almost elevated mendacity to the rank of a virtue.' This last assertion had reference to the catch saying at the General Election,

B

that if the labourers voted Liberal they would get 'Three acres and a cow.'

It is not easy to discover who was the originator of this saying, but it is probable that the custom on Lord Tollemache's Cheshire estate of giving three acres of land with each cottage, so prominently brought before the Royal Commission on the Housing of the Working Classes by Mr. F. Impey, Hon. Secretary of the Allotments Extension Association, gave the idea that any plan for improving the condition of the agricultural labourer would assume the form of an allotment sufficient to enable him to keep a cow.

There can be no doubt that Lord Tollemache has devoted a long lifetime to the careful management of his property both in Cheshire and Suffolk, and has done so with special regard to the comfort and interests of all resident on the estates or dependent on him ; Lord Tollemache has himself said that it has constituted his chief pleasure throughout life. While in no way desirous of detracting from the chorus of public approval with which his lordship's estate management has been greeted, it must be remarked that Lord Tollemache's Cheshire estate affords special facilities in this direction; but it would be unfair to many landlords were it not stated that on many other estates where equal facilities are found the system has been equally carried out. His property is situated in the centre of a first-class dairy district, where there is abundance of old pasture land and a population well skilled in, and able to appreciate the advantages of, dairy work; but it should not therefore be assumed that, because on other estates in the less fortunate districts of England the labourers have not three acres and a cow, it is on account of a refusal on the part of the owners of those estates to give facilities for the purpose. On the contrary, the words used by Mr. Chamberlain in his speech at Warrington, in reference to Lord Tollemache and Lord Carrington, viz. that 'they have, to the great advantage of their tenants and the great honour of themselves, adopted the system which I have advocated,' apply equally well to a host of other landlords.

Again, Mr. Chamberlain stated at Hull that great landlords have driven the labourers off their properties, partly in order to throw the land into immense farms; and another gentleman, representing a body of very radical land reformers, writes to the 'Daily News,' to the effect that the labourers have been, and still are, almost everywhere denied the secure and permanent use of the land on fair terms; while he holds up for commendation landlords like Lord Tollemache and '*a very few others.*'

In order to place the real state of the case fairly before the public, and that Parliament may not be called upon to pronounce an opinion upon this subject from the evidence of a few gentlemen whose knowledge on the subject must necessarily be limited to

the areas in which they have prosecuted their inquiries, an Association has been formed, entitled the
Land and Glebe Owners' Association for the Voluntary
Extension of the Allotments System, consisting of landowners and beneficed clergy in every part of England.

This Association has received an amount of support
which justly entitles it to represent the opinion of the
landowning classes in England ; its inquiries have been
confined to the latter country and those parts of Wales
which are not of so mountainous a character as to be
unsuitable for farming operations.

The Association has been formed for the purpose of
collecting evidence from residents in the country who
have access to, and special knowledge of, facts connected
with the management of large estates, and has two
objects in view. The first, to show the history and
existing state of the practice of letting small portions
of arable or pasture land to labourers who, not being
dependent for their living on their holdings, look to
regular wages as their chief means of livelihood, and
consider the allotment as a means of adding, in their
leisure hours, to the scanty comforts of the village
home. Secondly, to secure the adhesion of the greatest
possible number of land and glebe owners to the prin-
ciples of the Association, of which the main point is an
extension of the system to all labourers on their estates
who may desire to rent an allotment.

To this end a series of questions were submitted to

the larger landowners, the most important of which
invited an assurance from each that he is (1) prepared
to make proof to the public that he has taken, or will
take, steps to meet fully the demand for allotments
in his neighbourhood, and that he is (2) disposed to
facilitate the extension of the system to the agricultural
labourers employed on his estates.

A list of those who replied in the affirmative to
these questions will be found at the end of this book.

In addition to this, a number of owners have fur-
nished full particulars of the practice on their estates,
but accompanied with a request that they may not be
published. Much of this matter would be most interesting to the public, as demonstrating the concern
exhibited by such large landowners as the Duke of
Bedford, the Duke of Cleveland, and many others;
but I am, of course, bound to respect their wishes, and
confine myself only to such information concerning
the estates of these as has already been placed before
Parliament. Others who had willingly consented to
furnish evidence of the manner in which for years past
they have facilitated these tenures, after the recent
debate and division in the House of Commons, when
that part of the hitherto ' unauthorised programme ' of
the Liberal party dealing with the compulsory expro-
priation of landowners was accepted by the majority of
the House, wrote to me requesting that their names
might be removed from the list of those who had

accepted the undertaking entered into by members of the Association, and expressed an intention to bind themselves in no way further than to discharge, as they believed they always had done, their duty towards those connected with their estates. Every effort has been made to ensure exactitude in these returns, and in each case a proof has been sent to the owner with a request that he will himself make any alteration which may be necessary to secure perfect accuracy.

So far from there being anything new in the practice of granting land in allotments, we find that it is older than the century.

As far back as the year 1770 the lord of the manor of some commonable lands, near Tewkesbury, observing that the occupants of certain cottages to which some land was annexed were remarkable for their superior neatness and decency to others in the same neighbour-hood to whose cottages no land was attached, set out twenty-five acres for the use of the poor. The success was most marked; even those who before had been idle and profligate took an industrious turn, and the poor-rates of the parish were reduced to 4d. in the pound, as against 2s. 6d. to 5s. in adjoining parishes.

The industry of carding wool, followed by many women and children in the neighbourhood of Tetbury, died out about the year 1795; and Mr. Sotheron Estcourt, having occasion to stub out an overgrown gorse cover, divided that work among the labourers, allowing each one, after he had finished his allotted task, to rent the land cleared, as an occupation for himself and his family during odd hours.

In 1796 the state of the labourer attracted the attention of several influential persons, by whom a society was formed for 'bettering the condition and improving the comforts of the poor.' Of this society King George III. was patron. Reports were published from time to time till 1814, from which it appears that they considered one of the principal elements of success to be the 'allotments of land to the labouring population.'

In the year 1810, on Lord Winchilsea's estates, there were from seventy to eighty labourers who kept from one to four cows each.

The practice, however, did not become general till after the severe agricultural distress in 1830. In that year meetings were held all over the country to suggest and discuss measures for the relief of the able-bodied poor, &c., and a number of noblemen and gentlemen, 'to meet the pressing exigencies of the times,' formed a society called the 'Labourers' Friend Society,' having more especially for its object the obtaining a small portion of land for the labourer 'at a moderate rent in addition to the fair price of his labour.'

The founder of the society was Mr. Benjamin Wills, and the more prominent members of it were the Duke of Bedford, Lords Bute, Bristol, Shrewsbury,

Chichester, Euston, M.P., Jermyn, M.P., Morpeth, M.P.; Dacre, Sherborne, Kenyon, Gage, Foley, Ashtown, Skelmersdale, Nugent, and Mount-Sandford; the Bishops of Bath, Gloucester, Rochester, and Lichfield. It flourished for several years. Branches were established in different parts of the country, of which I can only trace one (the Chard and Crewkerne branch) still in existence.

One of these formed in the western division of the county of Surrey had for its object 'to call attention to the great advantage of the allotment system, and to furnish hints and give assistance to those who were willing to accept it.' This society reported that before it began its operations there were 400 allotments in twenty-four parishes. In Compton all were in full employment, and thirty-two heads of families had allotments. In West Horsley all cottages had gardens of from a quarter to one acre. In East Clandon twenty-one cottagers had half an acre of land, besides garden; and eight, enough meadow-land to keep a cow. In the years which succeeded its establishment a considerable increase was observed in the number of allotments let throughout its district.

Some societies, such as the West Suffolk, managed by Sir H. Bunbury, included in the sphere of its work the hiring of land on lease for the purpose of underletting as allotments.

From almost the beginning of the century it has

been sought to extend the allotment system by legislation, and many Acts have been passed with that object.

These Acts may be classed under three heads :—

I. Acts on the lines of the poor law, which give the parish authorities power to let land to the poor inhabitants to be cultivated by them on their own account. Acts of this class were passed in 1819 and 1831. They not only apply to land already held by the parish, but authorise the purchase of other land and the enclosure of wastes for the purpose of letting in allotments.

II. Inclosure Acts. Provisions for the establishment of allotment gardens for the poor, as a compensation for the loss of the advantages they enjoyed on the open waste, are to be found in a private Inclosure Act so far back as 1806, and the practice of giving compensation in this form soon became usual. By the General Inclosure Act, 1845, it was sought to enforce it in all suitable cases, and The Commons Act of 1876, while checking inclosure in general, supplements the deficiencies of the Act of 1845, and makes further and better provision for the allotment of suitable and sufficient land for field-gardens.

III. By Acts passed in 1832 and 1882 provision is made for the conversion into allotments for the poor of land held by parish dole-charities, and land in any other manner appropriated for the general benefit of the poor of any parish, and the Act of 1882 further provides that in any scheme to be thereafter made in

relation to any charity endowed with land, a portion
of the land should be set apart for allotments.

It does not appear that much advantage has been
taken of the first class of these Acts. Instances of their
application are or were to be found at Saffron Walden,
at Caunton, in Nottinghamshire, and at Battersea.

Under the General Inclosure Acts some 2,500 acres
in all have been allotted as field-gardens; since 1876
there have been only twenty-one commons enclosed,
and the amount allotted as field-gardens has been only
301 acres, but the average quantity so allotted on each
enclosure has been much larger than before.

The Act of 1832 was in its terms compulsory, but
it is believed there were not many cases where it
was applied. One instance is at Walton-on-Thames.
The Allotments Extension Act of 1882, however, has
already been put in force in a great number of places,
though the peculiarly stringent and compulsory nature
of its provisions causes considerable difficulties in its
application.

These Acts are only designed to supplement the
voluntary action of individuals. There is no compulsory
interference with the land of private owners. Even
the Act of 1882 only applies to lands used for public
purposes and managed by public bodies.

The material provisions of these and other Acts,
as well as of some Bills which failed to pass, are set
out and considered in detail in the latter part of this
book, together with some short chapters on the law

relating to the letting and management of allotments by private owners as well as under the special Acts, and a collection of precedents and forms.

One of the first corporate towns to avail itself of the provisions of the Act of 1819 was Saffron Walden, and a statement of the steps then taken may prove interesting.

In the year 1829, at a time when very great distress prevailed, a general meeting of the inhabitants of Saffron Walden was held, to consider what could best be done to ameliorate the condition of the labouring class. Lord Braybrooke presided, and the meeting was attended by the mayor, several members of the corporation, and many of the parishioners. Amongst other resolutions the following was unanimously adopted :

' That, both to encourage the industrious labourer and to try the experiment of whether or not land can be tilled on the parish account with benefit to the parochial funds, the said committee be authorised to hire a parcel or parcels of land not exceeding in the whole twenty acres (the quantity then limited by Act of Parliament), and to apportion any part thereof in small allotments at an equitable rent, to be let to the labouring poor having families or otherwise, as may be deemed advisable, and to appropriate the residue to the purposes of tillage, for the growth of potatoes, pulse, &c., on the parish account ; and that, in order to stimu-

late the landholders in the parish to offer ground for
this purpose, the proportion to be paid by them to the
parochial officers, on account of work actually done, be
two-fifths of the outlay per rod.'

The committee commenced their proceedings by
giving public notice that they were desirous of receiving
applications from those inhabitants who might wish
to have their land dug instead of ploughed, and also
that they were ready to hire portions of land not
exceeding in the whole twenty acres, under the provisions of the Act 59 Geo. III. cap. 12, with a view to
letting allotments to the poor.

Sixteen landholders availed themselves of the opportunity afforded them. Fifty-two acres of land were dug
by the parochial labourers at apportioned rates varying
from 2d. to 4d. per rod, the landholder being charged
for the work at the rate of from 16s. to 21s. 4d. per
acre ; and, as a result, the industrious labourer obtained,
in return for actual and profitable labour, a rate of
remuneration commensurate with the exertion made,
and considerably beyond that usually earned on the
public roads.

The experiment whether land could be cultivated
with advantage on the parish account was not tried,
as the applications for allotments were so numerous
that the whole of the land acquired by the committee
was devoted to this more desirable object.

The co-operation of some of the principal land-

owners and members of the corporation in letting plots
of ground to the cottagers, under the control of the
committee, without the intervention of the parochial
authorities, afforded facilities for extending the system,
and during the following year the area so applied was
increased to 33 A. 3 R. 9 P., divided into 157 plots, which
were let to 144 holders. It was estimated that upwards
of 700 persons were thus interested in and deriving
benefit from the undertaking.

In the year 1834 the attention of the Poor Law
Commissioners was called to the subject, and in their
report for that year (February 21) they state: 'The
immediate advantage of allotments is so great, that if
there were no other mode of supplying them, we think
it would be worth while, as a temporary measure, to
propose some general plan for providing them.' They
go on, however, to say, 'A labouring man, even when
his family is large, can seldom beneficially occupy more
than half an acre,' continuing to rely upon wages as his
regular and main support; and they pronounce strongly
against the use of the machinery of local authorities
for the purpose. They say, 'Where the system is carried on by individuals it has been generally beneficial,
but when managed by parish officers it has seldom
succeeded.'

About the year 1836, Mr. Henry Martin, of Hadlow
in Kent, advocated the introduction of the system into
that county, and stated that 3,000 families in the

county of Kent then occupied allotments. Sir George
Strickland in Yorkshire, Lord Chesterfield, the Duke
of Newcastle, and Lord Manners in Nottinghamshire, Lord Portman, Mr. Sturt, and Lord Rivers in
Dorsetshire, and other landowners in various parts of
the country, adopted the system previously to the
inquiry of 1843, and, as appears by the evidence, with
most satisfactory results.

In the years 1844 and 1845 Lord Mount Temple
(then Mr. Cowper) introduced a Bill to provide for the
election of field-wardens in every parish whose vestry
elected to adopt the Act, which gave power to the field-
wardens to rent land and relet it as allotments, giving
the security of the rates to the landowner for his rent.
The Bill was warmly supported by Sir James Graham
and the Government in the second session of its introduction, but did not succeed in passing into law.

The attention attracted by the discussion in
Parliament on this measure led to a great extension of
the system, and in 1867 a commission, appointed to
inquire into the employment of children, young persons, and women in agriculture, reported ' that the best
method by which the pecuniary condition of the agricultural labourer, where low, can be improved, and to
which the Legislature could give a salutary stimulus
by simple and unobjectionable means,' was ' a more
general adoption of the practice of attaching such an
amount of land to the labourer's cottage, or, in default
of that, in assigning to him such an amount of land

as near to his dwelling as possible, as will profitably employ the leisure hours of himself and his family without turning him into a small farmer, or leading him to place his chief dependence on the produce of his land, and not on wages.'

This Commission went very closely into the question of allotments to the labouring poor, as also did the Commission on Agriculture in 1882, and that on the Housing of the Working Classes in 1884-5; and from the evidence and reports of these Commissions much interesting information as to the practice on different estates is to be obtained. It is, however, greatly to be regretted that the strong recommendation of the Commission of 1867, that 'it would be highly desirable that a return of the quantity so allotted should be made from each agricultural parish; and such a return would probably be attainable, with very little additional trouble at the same time that the annual agricultural returns are collected by the officers of the Inland Revenue Department under direction of the Statistical Department of the Board of Trade,' should have only been very partially and intermittently complied with.

Lord Spencer, on behalf of the Government, has now promised an exhaustive return of all allotments attached and unattached to labourers' dwellings, in the latter case with the distance from the cultivator's home; also of all small holdings of pasture, together with the number of labourers who are allowed potatoe ground and run for a cow.

THE PRACTICE IN DIFFERENT COUNTIES.

THE practice of letting land to labourers differs so greatly in various parts of the country, that it will be advisable to take the counties, or, at any rate, groups of counties, separately, in order to show how far land-owners have met the labourers' desire for allotments of different kinds.

In the home counties, Kent is not so well provided with field gardens as some others, from the fact that the gardens attached to the cottages are unusually large. Lord Harris recently asked every labourer whether he would like a larger garden; very few expressed such a wish, but arrangements were immediately made to meet the wishes of those who did. Lord Radnor has granted a large quantity of land at Folkestone to be let in allotments of from ten perches to half an acre each in the vicinity of the Junction Railway Station, and there are already over 100 applicants. In Sussex allotments are general. The Rev. John Goring, of Wiston Park, has carried out the system of giving more land as the labourers were able to stock and farm it, until he has now upwards of thirty tenants with rents varying from 4*l.* to 60*l.* who were originally day labourers, and whose aggregate rental is 1,000*l.* a year. On Lord Egmont's estate there are 370 allotments. The late Lord Gage took the greatest interest in the subject, and was a warm supporter of the Labourers' Friend Society. The agent to his Firle estate says that arable allotments are in excess of the demand, though he thinks that pasture allotments, so long as they do not interfere with the labourer's work on a farm, might be advantageous to him, and he intends to try this plan at Michaelmas next.

In Surrey the fruits of the Labourers' Friend Society remain in the fact that hardly a village is without its allotment-ground. On Mr. Cubitt's estate, near Dorking, a large field has been set apart and handed over to a committee of tradesmen of the town to let as a garden-ground to the poorer inhabitants.

In Hampshire, Mr. Little reports that allotments are let at about 32*s.* an acre, and the county was well supplied with them in 1867. On Lord Winchester's Amport estates a committee of the allotment-holders appointed by themselves settles the amount of compensation to be paid by the incoming to the outgoing tenant, and his lordship's agent is of opinion that, provided the men were of known good character, the duty of deciding on the compensation to be paid by the land-lord in any case of disturbance in the holding might be fairly entrusted to the same body. The rental in

C

this county is very low; on Lord Mount Temple's estate
lower than that of land of equal value let in farms.
Mr. Chamberlayne, of Cranbury, who owns land on the
outskirts of Southampton, is devoting a large area to
allotments, not only for labouring men but also for
artisans and tradesmen.

In Wiltshire there is no lack of allotments, though
Lord Pembroke, who has 900 on his estate, thinks that
there is still room for extension. He says: 'I think
I may go so far as to say that I believe the allotment
system might be extended. Hitherto it has perhaps
been regarded by landlords and agents rather as a
benefit to labourers than a matter of business and
profit, as I think it might become. However this may
be, the allotment system exists and is growing here,
and in many other parts of the country.' This is
evidenced by the action of Mr. Hussey Freke, who is
at the present moment laying out land for the purpose
adjoining the town of Highworth. Mr. Druce reports
that the average rental is 5d. a perch. On the
Marquess of Ailesbury's estates it appears that there
are 268 acres and 39 poles, divided into 973 allotments,
varying from 20 to over 100 lugs (poles) each. Nor is
this by any means exceptional. On the contrary, the
agent, Mr. Woolcott, says : ' Such allotments exist more
or less on almost every other similar estate within
my knowledge, and I submit this as a fair sample
of such holdings on large estates.' The late Lord

Carnarvon, writing in 1830, said: 'In a parish in Wilts, of which I am the principal proprietor, I have very nearly arrived at the point at which every cottager will be the occupant of a sufficient portion of land to raise vegetables for his family and enough to fatten his pig.'

Writing in the 'Nineteenth Century,' Lord Nelson says: 'Let me give a short account of how my small holdings have been formed. In one parish I asked the farmer of a 400-acre farm to give up forty acres near the village for allotments; this he did gradually, as he had taken the wheat crop off the land. It is now let to eighty-five tenants in portions varying from twenty perches to two acres apiece, fifteen having over an acre, at a rent of 3*l.* an acre. Losing 2 acres 1 rood 22 poles in paths and roadways, I get, after paying 24*l.* for rates and taxes, about 2*l.* an acre. The men who have it do not grumble; there are hardly ever vacant allotments, and though outsiders say the rent should only be 1*l.* instead of 3*l.*, I well know, if I sold it in two-acre pieces for building purposes, I could easily get 100*l.* an acre for the land.'

'In another parish, on a farm in the middle of the parish being given up, I divided it into cow-land, fencing and building cowsheds, paying rates and taxes, and giving the tenant the permanent grasses to lay it down in pasture where not already meadow land. Part of another farm, about forty acres, falling in, I similarly

divided it in agricultural allotments to four tenants, as
it was also within easy reach of the village.'

On Sir George Jenkinson's property, in 1856, fifty-six
acres were let out in allotments of one-third of an acre
to each tenant, all of which at the time was taken, and
in 1863 about eleven acres more were added, and as the
population was scattered over a wide area, portions of
eleven different fields, situated as near as possible to
the homes of the tenants, were chosen. For these they
were charged at the rate of $3\frac{1}{2}d$. per perch, in every case
the landlord paying all tithes, rates, taxes, and expenses.
All went tolerably well for some years, but since agricultural wages have risen and the price of corn has been
so low, ten and a half acres out of the forty-eight have
been given up and taken in hand; about three acres more
are now unoccupied, and about twelve acres have been
let to persons—in most cases small tradesmen—who
had an allotment before.

In Berkshire Mr. Little stated to the Commission
on Agriculture that allotment rents were in some
cases higher than other land, but the average run was
$3d$. to $6d$. per perch. On Sir Richard Sutton's estate
every labourer can have an allotment if he desires.
At Wantage, where so much has been done to provide land for small holders by the present Lord
Wantage, there was, in 1854, a society called 'The
Wantage Society for providing the Poor with Land.'
Out of thirty-five allotment-holders the society reported

that in the first year eighteen cultivated their allotments well, six rather more than well, six very well indeed, four in a 'middling' manner, and only one badly.

In Buckinghamshire, on Lord Carrington's estate, allotments are very numerous; but till recently the rent was high, which led to some disinclination to take them. Since a reduction has been made they are as popular as ever. At Steeple Claydon, Sir Harry Verney, Bart., has set apart seven acres of Stifflands Farm, to be let in garden allotments of one quarter acre at 10s. to the cottagers of the parish, who hitherto had to walk some two miles to their allotments. The land is let on the condition that only vegetables shall be grown upon it. Lord Rothschild's allotments are lower than the adjoining farmland. Near Henley, on the borders of Berkshire, there is but little demand. Mr. Mackenzie, of Fawley Court, offered 200 acres close to the town, and had but few applications. But in the more rural parts the system is on the increase, for the Duke of Buckingham finds that he can obtain occupiers for land which his farm-tenants are now surrendering for the purpose. Where there is any difficulty the farmers, says Mr. Druce, give potato ground.

The Western counties are exceptionally well supplied with allotments. In Dorsetshire, Lord Alington, in addition to his own allotments, has hired land in a more suitable situation, and sublet it, at a loss to him-

self, in 144 allotments. Close to Blandford land lets
at the rate of 2*l.* an acre. General Pitt Rivers, who
inherited Lord Rivers' estates, says there have been
allotments on the estate for many years, and he is willing
to continue to grant them not only to labourers on the
estate but to all who desire them; while Mr. Farqu-
harson, the Member for the Western Division, is daily
extending the system. The late Lord Sherborne, who
took much interest in the question, drew up the first
rules on record for the letting of allotment land about
the year 1840. They provided—

1. That the entry should be on November 15, and
notice be given on August 1.

2. That the incoming tenant, where notice had
been given, should enter to plant his winter crops on
August 1.

3. That each tenant should keep one pig, and not
grow the same crop on the same land two years in
succession.

4. That there should be no underletting.

5. That no labour should be done on the allotment
during the hours of farm labour without the master's
consent.

6. That the rent should be paid within ten days of
November 15.

7. That conviction of crime should be followed by
forfeiture.

Devonshire is another of the counties where the allotment system may be said to be carried almost to perfection. Sir Thomas Dyke Acland, who has ever taken the greatest interest in the welfare of those on his estate, has in Broadclyst 250 allotments in twenty-four different places, varying from twenty to forty perches. The total rent paid for fifty-five and a half acres is 127*l.* 8*s.* The expenses and outgoings are 44*l.*, leaving net rental 83*l.*, or 30*s.* per acre. The allotments are occupied by 170 agricultural labourers, 48 mechanics, 6 tradesmen, 10 gardeners, and 18 widows and other persons. The rents have been unchanged for half a century, though the time of entry has been altered to November.

Sir Thomas has also a number of allotments, close to the town of South Molton, let to 113 tenants, and as this gentleman has long been identified with liberal views on the Land question, I shall perhaps be pardoned if I refer to his allotments at some length, as tending to show the misconception which exists on the subject of the rent of accommodation land when let in allotments.

The rent of these allotments is nominally 9*d.* per perch or 7*s.* 6*d.* per annum, but 1*s.* 6*d.* is given back on punctual payment, which reduces the rent to about 7¼*d.* per perch, or 6*s.* a year.

The return per acre is therefore 4*l.* 16*s.* gross, but

as the outgoings, which the lessor pays, amount to
18s. 6d. per acre, the net rent is 3l. 17s. 6d. per acre.
The fields immediately contiguous to two of the allotment fields are let as accommodation land at rents of
about 5l. per acre, the tenants paying the outgoings.
If compared with these fields, the allotment lands
cannot be said to be highly rented, but one of them
adjoins a farm, and the allotment tenants seem to
think that they ought not to pay proportionately more
than the average rent of the farm, about 1l. per acre.

Inquiries were made as to the rents of other allotments in South Molton, and it was found that some are
let at 1s., others at 9d., those of the Town Council at
4½d. per perch.   The quality and aspect of the two
former are about equal to those of Sir Thomas Acland,
and that of the Council inferior. The Council allotments,
though let at a lower rate than any of the others, are
not fully taken up, owing to the exposed situation and
lower quality of the field.   The supply, therefore, may
be said to be more than sufficient for the demand, and it
is open to any applicant who declines to give the price
asked by Sir Thomas Acland to take land of the Council.
A holder on the Acland estate of more than forty years'
standing states that the allotment, if properly managed,
will yield a fair return, and calculates that the crops
following the potato crop should pay his rent and other
expenses, leaving the potato crop as nett profit.   He
estimated his expenses as follows :—

	£	s.	d.
Rent	0	6	0
Manure	0	10	6
Labour	0	15	0
	1	11	6

He grew a bag of potatoes a yard this season which would bring him in from 35s. to 40s.; the after-crop would be sufficient to pay expenses. This man said he was quite satisfied with his rent.

The Hon. Mark Rolle for many years past has had on his property twenty-two allotment fields varying from one to twelve acres, and making up an aggregate of about one thousand acres, let to nearly one thousand tenants. The average size of the allotment is an eighth of an acre, and the rent, from 5s. to 6s. 8d., is paid in advance in January in each year. Mr. Mark Rolle is of the opinion that twenty perches is the most that a working man can find manure for and can cultivate after working hours, seeing that most of the allotment tenants have, in addition, gardens attached to their cottages. Mr. Rolle says that it is his wish to extend the system on his estates. On a neighbouring estate, that of Lord Clinton, where the allotments amount to a quarter or half an acre each, the improvement in the condition of the labourer has been still more marked.

In Cornwall, the high wages received by miners lead them to disregard any offers of allotments, though many seem to like, as on Hon. Mrs. Gilbert's estate, to

occupy a few acres of grass land.   The rule in the county
appears to be to give good gardens with the cottages.

In Staffordshire the Commissioners of 1867 reported that allotments were not uncommon.   Mr.
Doyle says the practice is only partial, the reason being
that wages are high and the labourers do not care for
allotments.

In Warwickshire, however, allotments are greatly
appreciated.   Near Birmingham, Lord Norton gives
every able-bodied cottager a quarter of an acre of land,
and has a system of increasing the holding to half an
acre, one acre, and upwards, as the occupier can show
that he is accumulating sufficient money to stock and
work his allotment.   Lord Hertford has been increasing his allotments since 1882, and is now cutting up
more land in the same way.

In Northamptonshire there were, in 1873, as the
Parliamentary Return shows, a larger number of allotments than in any county in England.   Mr. Druce says
the ordinary rent is 3*d*. to 6*d*. a pole.   Lord Henley
says that in some places there are complaints that the
allotments are left in a bad state of cultivation, but,
in his forty years' experience of the system, he has
himself rarely met with cases of bad cultivation.

Lord Spencer is about to try a new plan with
regard to the cultivation of small holdings.   The
profits of a farm of 300 acres are to go to the
labourers after paying 4 per cent. on the capital,

which Lord Spencer will provide. The choice of the
labourers who are to work the farm has been made
from the inhabitants by ballot. There are to be eight
men on the farm and one manager. All the details
are to be settled by the men themselves, who are to
receive wages at the rate of 14s. per week, and divide
the profits over and above the 4 per cent. to be repaid
to Lord Spencer.

In Worcestershire and Hereford allotments do not
appear to be very common, probably because the land
in those counties is chiefly devoted to fruit-culture.
On Sir H. F. Vernon's estate allotments are let, and
the trees are supplied to the tenant; the rent remains
the same as that of land let in farms plus the amount
of all outgoings; at the expiration of five years, when
the trees begin to bear, an additional rent has to be paid,
which is calculated to repay the sum expended by the
landlord in fruit-trees; after this there is no further
increase. The land is of exceptionally good quality
for fruit-growing, and close to a railway station. In
other cases, where the tenant finds the trees, he acquires,
by the custom of the country, a tenant-right in his
holding. Gardens close to the town of Wellington
have been let as high as 8l. an acre, while within a
quarter of a mile of the same town allotments sometimes go begging at 64s. an acre, with 16s. rates and
taxes paid by the landlord.

In Monmouthshire nearly every cottage has an

excellent garden. Some freehold land societies have been formed in Monmouth and other towns during the last twenty years, and the members have acquired small freeholds, but, with few exceptions, they have not been profitable. Many of the labourers have from one to five or six acres of land, paying very moderate rents, and in some cases, as in Trelleck Manor, where the tenure is peculiar, the rents are merely nominal. Much of the land in Trelleck and Usk Manors was at one time common land, on which the ancestors of the present occupiers built cottages.

Gloucestershire, as has been already stated, may be called the cradle of allotments, for in this county are the Tewkesbury and Tetbury allotments of the last century. These 'poor's plots,' as they were afterwards called, exist in nearly every village, though many are being given up, owing to the bad times, and the following experiment, tried by Sir Michael Hicks-Beach, shows how little they are now sought after.

Notice in the following terms was posted in the village shop:—

'Any householder in Coln St. Aldwyns, desirous to rent a piece of land of from one to six acres, can learn from Mr. G. N. Woolley, Coln Lower Mill, the terms on which it would be let. Early application is necessary.'

The following instructions were given as to the letting :—

'It will be necessary for applicants to show—

' 1. That they are able to command a certain amount of money, say at the rate of 3*l*. per acre.

' 2. That their gardens or allotments are well cultivated, and their rents not in arrear.

' The land will be let free of tithe, rates, and taxes.

' Rents to be paid half-yearly; and some simple provisions against exhaustion by over-cropping agreed to.

' If three acres are taken the rent will be 25*s*. or 20*s*. per acre, according to situation.

' For a piece of less than three acres a rather higher rent per acre will be charged; above three acres, rather less ; in each case in proportion to the acreage.

' As each of the fields proposed comprises between seventeen and eighteen acres, no promise can be made to give it up for this purpose, unless there should be a sufficient number of qualified applicants to take it all between them.

' But if one or two applications only should be made, Sir M. Hicks-Beach would try to meet them in the present allotment-ground.'

Not a single application for land was made, though the parish contains a population of 430 of all classes.

Near Cheltenham there is an estate of some 200 acres, divided into cottage-holdings of from eight to thirty acres of pasture land, let at 2*l*. to 2*l*. 10*s*. per acre. They were established by Mr. Booth Grey, a brother of Lord Stamford, some eighty years ago. The result is

most successful, and the village of 350 inhabitants is a
model one.

In the Midland grazing counties the field garden
and allotment system—viz. the letting of small portions
of arable land—is almost unknown, as shown by the returns published in 1873 by the Agricultural Department
of the Privy Council, who state that in the two great
pasture counties of Cheshire and Derbyshire only twenty-
eight acres were so let.

In Cheshire, it is perhaps needless to speak of Lord
Tollemache's well-known estate further than to say that a
similar practice of allowing farm-labourers to hire three
acres or more obtains on many estates in the county.
For some time Lord Crewe has been increasing the
number of small holdings on his estates in Cheshire
and over the border in North Staffordshire. Land has
been distributed in various quantities, and agricultural
rentals only charged. For instance, numerous commo-
dious three-roomed cottages, with large and productive
gardens attached, have been provided for farm-labourers
at the rental of 4l. 10s. per annum; cottage farms,
with suitable dwellings, outbuildings, gardens, and from
two to three acres of land each, are also let to labourers
at from 8l. to 10l. per annum, and the earnings and
home comforts of these men compare favourably with
those of higher-class artisans in the towns. Lord
Crewe has now no fewer than 195 tenants holding half
an acre and under three acres, 144 with three and

under ten acres, 30 with ten and under twenty acres,
31 with twenty and under fifty acres, 40 with fifty and
under a hundred acres, 41 with a hundred and under
two hundred acres, and 14 only over two hundred and
under five hundred acres.

The Duke of Westminster has 354 tenants, holding
as follows :—

Tenants without allotments.	.	. 257	}	354
„ with allotments	.	. 97		
„ cowkeepers	.	. 182	}	354
„ without cows .	.	. 172		
„ without cows or allotments	.	. 130	}	354
„ with one or other	.	. 224		
Summary of holdings under 1 acre	.	. 236		
„ „ 1 to 5 acres	.	. 87		
„ „ 5 to 10 „	.	. 31]		

Lord Harrington lets many allotments, which are
chiefly in the occupation of the Macclesfield weavers.

The neighbouring county of Shropshire has much
in common with Cheshire. Sir Baldwyn Leighton's
father commenced the practice half a century ago,
and it is described in Mr. Stanhope's report to the
Commissioners on Employment in Agriculture. The
present baronet has advocated the system publicly and
in print for the last twenty years; several of his
labourers' families have been on the same plot for
more than a generation. Some fourteen years ago, Sir
Baldwyn, addressing a Birmingham audience, surprised
his hearers by a statement of these facts, and it is not

unlikely that the recent agitation has tardily arisen from his remarks.

On Mr. Jasper More's estate there are eighty-four tenants holding under fifteen acres each, and a similar system is in operation on the estates of the Duke of Cleveland, Lord Forester, and Lord Hill. On Colonel Edwards' estate, of which so much has been said in the publications of the Allotments and Small Holdings Association, and to which I shall have occasion to refer hereafter, there are, besides the large farm tenancies, nearly twenty holdings of thirteen acres and under occupied by labourers, or small village tradesmen embracing almost every vocation of the country side. During the past eight years there have been no arrears, and the occupiers themselves declared they needed no reductions.

In Derbyshire arable allotments are but little sought after, but 'cowleys,' as they are called, are common. Here, as in Lord Stanley's park in Cheshire, where ninety-eight cottagers, artisans, &c. and seventy-three farmers run 'ley' cattle, the Duke of Devonshire takes in the labourer's cow to pasture in Chatsworth Park. The animals are usually allowed to run in the park from May till October, but sometimes they are kept on through the winter.

The Commission of 1867 stated that in Derbyshire all cottages belonging to landowners had either gardens attached to them or small allotments of garden-gronnd.

Allotments were also provided near many of the towns and mining villages, and were greatly prized by the miners and mechanics. Mr. Culley, the Assistant Commissioner, writing of the state of affairs nine years ago, says :—

'I believe it would be impossible to over-estimate the value of such a provision of milk as is within the reach of the families of most of the Derbyshire labourers.

'Many labourers in the North of Derbyshire rent with their cottages six or eight acres of grass land with a shippon attached, and are thus enabled to keep two cows during both summer and winter. Others rent a smaller quantity of grass land, which they mow, and graze their cows during summer in one of their master's fields, or more commonly in the nearest nobleman or gentleman's park. Others again, who live near a park where they can enjoy this privilege, and who have no cow of their own, borrow one from a farmer, and so get her milk for the summer months at a cost of from 3*l.* to 4*l.*

'Some further examples of the evidence received on this subject will perhaps explain the milk system better, and show how, in the opinion of persons who know both classes, a labourer with his cow-allotment compares with a small farmer.

'Mr. Cottingham, agent to the Duke of Devonshire, speaking of Edensor, says : " The cottages have all gardens, and most of them have sufficient land to winter

D

a cow. In summer they pasture their cows in Chatsworth Park, paying 3*l.* for the summer's grass, about
twenty-one weeks."

'On the subject of cow allotments *versus* small
farms, Mr. Cottingham says: "I think that a man
with an allotment of, say, ten acres, to keep a couple of
cows, is better off than the holder of twenty or thirty
acres or a farm just big enough to tempt him to do
nothing else but work on his farm. I reduced one man
to ten acres from twenty to compel him to work, and he
afterwards told me I had 'made a gentleman of him.'
He now works for the Duke of Devonshire at 14*s.* a
week, and has his grass allotment of ten acres. This
system works well, bringing up a good class of labourers,
and giving their wives an occupation at home."

'The Rev. J. Hall, Vicar of Edensor, says: "I am
clearly of opinion that the small farmers—*i.e.* persons
holding from thirty to sixty acres of land—are as a class
worse off in this neighbourhood than the labourers, who
receive generally from 14*s.* to 18*s.* per week. On the
other hand, where a labourer can have, as is common
with us, just as much grass land as will enable him to
keep one or two cows, which can be managed by his wife,
with scarcely any demand upon his own time, his position is undoubtedly much better than that of those to
whom this is denied. I am satisfied that these views
are shared by nearly all who are acquainted with the
district."'

'Mr. Samuel Turner, bailiff to the Duke of Devonshire for the Bakewell district, says: "We have a good many occupiers of a cottage and a few acres who keep one or two cows. These men are labourers as well, and are well off—fully as well off as a man who farms thirty acres and is not a regular farmer. A man who occupies less than 100 acres has great difficulty to make a living, as land here is chiefly grazing land. Men who have no land can 'ley' a cow for twenty weeks in summer for 4*l.*"'

In Nottinghamshire, the Commission of 1867 found that allotments were very common, and very cheaply let; in cases where they were let free, it was found that the independent spirit of the labourer took but little advantage of the eleemosynary benefit.

In Leicestershire, allotments were very common in 1867. On Lord Howe's estate cow pastures have long been in vogue. The Leicestershire cottages are in many cases built without gardens, close up to the road. On Sir Henry Halford's estate, land has been offered to any amount to labourers, but there are already allotments in every parish, and many are vacant. The tenants of the allotments grow corn, but at present prices they, like others engaged in farming, have reduced the acreage under that cereal. In 1844, in the parish of Croxton Kerrial, near Grantham, the late Duke of Rutland gave allotments for gardens to the labourers of the parish. There were forty-seven allotments, in the

D

middle of the parish, given entirely to the agricultural labourers. The population being about six hundred, the allotments provided gardens for nearly every labouring family in the parish. The Duke has in the parish of Croxton Kerrial over forty-one cow allotments, and a corresponding number of garden allotments on his property there.

Rutland is another of the pioneer counties in the creation of allotments, for Lord Winchelsea's cow allotments, already alluded to, were in this county. The Duke of Richmond's Commission reported that before the beginning of the century allotments were common, the average rental being twenty poles, let at a rent equal to or but slightly higher than farms.

From Cambridgeshire, Huntingdonshire, and Hertfordshire I have received comparatively few returns. The Duke of Manchester is very anxious to continue the development of the system on the Kimbolton estates, and in Hertfordshire Lord Salisbury informed me that allotments have existed ever since he can remember. It is proposed to form at once a branch of the Land and Glebe Owners' Association in this county, where the necessary organisation is already prepared. This example, it is hoped, will be shortly followed in all the agricultural counties of England.

In the northern counties, Northumberland, Durham, Cumberland, Westmoreland, and Lancashire very little demand for allotments exists, chiefly owing to

the high wages and to the fact that the practice generally obtains of hiring a labourer by the year only, at
the expiration of which time he may leave his master
and find himself engaged in quite a different part of
the county. Before the year 1867, Lord Sefton, whose
estates are not far from Liverpool, set aside a twenty-
five-acre field conveniently situated near a railway
station, and made it known that he would let small
lots of land of from a quarter to one acre, but he did
not receive a single application.

Many years ago one of the Dukes of Northumberland planted small villages upon his estate in Northumberland, his wish being to prevent if possible the
yearly emigration of farm servants, by making the
cottagers hold direct from the landlord, and not from
the farmer. Each cottage had a house with stable or
byre, gardens, and from five to ten acres of land attached, at a low rent. These cottages were planted in
small villages, and in clumps of two, three, or four, on
various farms over the estate. Of these small villages
and clumps of cottages, with the exception of two
or three places, all have now been absorbed into the
surrounding farms, and the houses and crofts have dis-
appeared. Of those that remain, the occupiers are generally shopkeepers, carriers, masons, and small tradesmen,
with very few labourers, thus proving that the experiment has failed and that the labouring man could not
live upon the small holding, and preferred the cottage

and garden at the farm to the rather large holding, for which he would pay rent.

At Wark-on-Tweed there are a number of ancient holdings which were originally those of old leaseholders, or retainers of the Castle of Wark, the dwellings being clustered round the old castle. They are now considered as customary freeholds, and pay rents from 3s. 9d. to 20s. to the lord of the manor. Each freeholder has a cottage with byre and garden attached, two or three plots of land within a short distance, and a cow's grass upon land set apart for that purpose. The original rents were 6d. a year, and the term for life, with an addition of a hen and capon each year. These seem to have been valued or commuted at 3s. 3d., making in money 3s. 9d.

In the year 1884 there were twenty-four only upon the books, the remainder having sold out to the lord of the manor. Of these twenty-four, fifteen were non-resident, and let their premises to other parties, and nine were resident and occupying their own premises. These comprised three labourers, two road-men (contractors), one tailor, one blacksmith, one joiner, one general dealer (grocer, &c.).

About thirty years ago, Alnwick Moor was enclosed and divided, and money was borrowed to fence and drain it. Each freeman was entitled to have for his life one acre of infield and three acres of outfield land, and these he held in right of his being a freeman, and free of rent except the instalments upon borrowed money and expenses of management. In 1878 the freeman valued these privileges at 6*l.* a year. In 1868, 286 one-acre allotments were held by freemen and freemen's widows; of these 124 were cultivated by the holders and 160 let to other parties. Much of this land, broken up for tillage under the award, has been badly managed by the holders, and is now going out of cultivation, exhausted and worn out, showing that the privilege in many instances is not appreciated, the returns from cultivation not being worth the trouble and expense. In some cases a few allotments are thrown together and rented by carters, who make a livelihood by carting for hire, and use these lands for keeping their horses.

The freemen of Berwick have certain rights to what are called stints and meadows. These consist of land, and are, or were, well-defined, and are worth from 5*l.* to 20*l.* a year, according to position and quality. The freemen can, if wished, occupy these themselves, but they are in almost every instance let. When let separately, some of the carters or small farmers generally take three or four or more, sufficient to enable them to cultivate and make a livelihood. In many instances large numbers of these holdings have been laid together and farms formed, upon which houses and homesteads have been built. The farms are let to tenants, and the rents divided among the freemen who represent these stints or meadows comprising the farms.

In Yorkshire, however, the custom flourishes, and is as greatly appreciated as in any other part of the kingdom. On Lord Herries' estate almost every labourer has his ' cow and three acres,' and the same is the case on the estates of Sir George Wombwell, consisting of 12,600 acres; nearly all the cottages in the villages of Coxwold, Oulston, Yearsley, and Old Byland have not less than three acres of grass, some more, let with them, and to every cottage is attached a cow-house and piggery, besides a good-sized garden adjoining the cottage. For the cottage and garden the labourer pays from 4l. to 5l. per annum, and for the cow-gait of three acres, 6l. per annum. This allotment system has been in operation on the Newburgh estates for eighty years, and Sir George Wombwell loses no opportunity of increasing it.

Cow clubs are in operation throughout this district, and in ordinary times are found to work well, but the subscription to the club only begins *after* a member has lost a cow; consequently, in case of a murrain or heavy loss of cows by the members, there are no funds to meet the calls on the club.

The plan adopted in some of these clubs is that, when a cow dies, each member pays 7s. a month to make up the 11l. required, which sum is collected by one of the members, who is called the ' pasture-master,' an office which changes every year; there is no further collection until the next cow dies. In other clubs they have a sum in the bank; when a cow dies, they pay to the member who has lost his cow the sum of 10*l.* out of the funds, and then they commence to collect again from each member 1*s.* per month until the full amount of the reserve fund is made up again.

The system has this advantage, that when a man loses a cow, he is not under the necessity of sending a subscription list round to his richer neighbours to obtain funds to replace his loss.

The best set of rules I have been able to find for a cow club are those on the estate of Mr. Heneage, the Chancellor of the Duchy of Lancaster, which will be found in the Appendix. By these rules, an entrance-fee and monthly subscription are required *before* the member suffers any loss, and precautions are also taken that the cows of the labourers admitted to membership are subjected to careful examination. Medical attendance and drinks are also provided in cases of illness.

One exists on Lord Tollemache's estate; the rules of the club given in Mr. Evershed's (of Hurstmonceux) contribution to the publications of the Royal Agricultural Society on ' Cow-keeping by Labourers,' a reprint of which may be obtained of the author, provide for the establishment of a club-house, but to this club the larger farmers are also admitted to membership.

Arable allotments do not seem popular in Yorkshire, as Lord Wenlock did not receive a single application in response to his offer to provide allotments in an arable field.

Mr. Portman, reporting to the Commissioners of 1867, says: 'In one part of the county, at least, the advantages enjoyed by the Yorkshire agricultural labourers generally in yearly hirings, high weekly wages, opportunities of piecework, and good gardens attached to their cottages, or allotments in default of them, are, according to the evidence of the Rev. S. Surtees, made good use of towards securing a provision for old age. Mr. Surtees says that near Doncaster it is the rule, and not the exception, for a labourer to leave at his death 50*l.* to 100*l.*, and he quotes a case of one man who commenced life as a farm servant, and had brought up and started a family in life, who left 350*l.*; another, who died at thirty-five years of age, an ordinary agricultural labourer, leaving 170*l.* These are, no doubt, special instances; but, considering the high rate of wages in Yorkshire, the almost universal possession by the labourer of a garden or allotment, and in many cases of a cow-gait or other advantages, there is no reason to doubt that a man commencing life as a farm servant and exercising ordinary prudence can, by the assistance of a savings' bank, lay up a fair provision for his old age.'

In Oxfordshire there were, in 1867, 914 allotments on the Duke of Marlborough's estate, and 9,088 in that county in 1873.

A reprint of the Commissioner's report upon the O'Connor allotments at Minster, which, it should be borne in mind, was written at a time when agricultural produce commanded a far higher price than it does in 1886, may not be uninteresting.

In the year 1847 (about the same time that he purchased some other estates for the same purpose), Mr. Fergus O'Connor purchased an estate of about 300 acres in Minster Lovell parish on behalf of the shareholders of his land company. This estate he divided into eighty-five allotments of from two to four acres each (thirty-six of them being four acres), and built a cottage on each allotment, distributing the plots of ground with their cottages amongst those of the shareholders of the land company who had paid up the full amount of a share in the order in which they stood upon his list. When a shareholder obtained possession of his little farm he received from the funds of the company 'head money' at the rate of 7l. 10s. an acre, and was charged with his share of the interest of a mortgage debt of 5,000l. To use the language of Mr. Freer, who now owns about one-third of the estate, 'as long as the head-money lasted all went well,' but in a few years many of the allottees, who were chiefly artisans from large towns, left their allotments, and the interest of the debt not being paid, the mortgagees offered the estate and newly-built cottages for sale; the mortgagees were, however, unable to effect a sale, and the state of affairs having been brought before the House of Commons, the estate was handed over to the

Court of Chancery, which, on October 6, 1851, appointed
an official manager to wind up the affairs of the land
company. The result of the winding-up was that a
considerable number of the allotments were sold, and
the possession of the remainder was confirmed to the
allottees on payment of a rent-charge, which in the
case of a four-acre allotment amounted to 9*l.* 10*s.*, a
tolerably fair farm-rent (allowing 3*l.* for the cottage),
though such an allotment, subject to the rent-charge,
can now be sold for upwards of 100*l.* When the Commissioner visited the Charterville in October, 1867, he
found only two of the original allottees in possession of
their cottages and ground, and one of these was not
strictly in possession, as his allotment had just been
sold. This man's evidence was as follows :—

'Those that paid up a whole share got the first
choice of an allotment. I paid up mine, 5*l.* 7*s.* 6*d.* I
got one in six months. I never would if I had known
what I do now. It has taken me twenty years to
learn how a man can live without victuals, and I have
just about come to it. Thousands paid up part of
their share and lost it all, and I believe they were best
off. I got 30*l.* head-money for four acres. My allotment has been sold for 106*l.*, but there is a rent-charge
on it of 9*l.* 10*s.* a year.'

In Bedfordshire, Mr. Druce reports that the custom
is very general to let allotments at the ordinary agricultural value. On the Duke of Bedford's estate the

allotments are from twenty poles to a quarter of an acre, and are in addition to gardens. Mr. Wing states that the Duke of Bedford, who owns 1,116 modern-built cottages, has a great anxiety gradually to attach allotments to all the cottages; in fact, to enlarge the gardens, because in so many instances the allotments are at a distance from the cottages. On the Duke's estates in Beds and Bucks there are 1,204 allotments, five farms under fifty acres and fourteen under 100. On his Grace's Cambridgeshire, Northamptonshire, and Huntingdonshire estates there are 414 allotments, seventeen farms under fifty and six under 100 acres; on his estates in Devon, Cornwall, and Dorset there are 479 allotments, fourteen farms under fifty acres and eighteen under 100.

On the estates of Mr. Charles Magniac, M.P., every tenant, with one or two exceptions, has a garden, and in addition an allotment, for which they pay from 20s. to 33s. an acre. All the men were called together some two years ago and told they might have as much more land as they wished for, and had means to cultivate, at the same rate as adjacent farms. Not a single application was made for more.

I have purposely deferred any description of allotments in the Eastern counties till the last because the variety and extent of the allotment-holdings are greater than in any other part of England; and, also, because it is in these counties that attention has chiefly been directed to an alleged demand for allotments.

Lincolnshire is the county in which exist the small freeholds of Axholm, of which so much has been lately said and written that it will be unnecessary to do more than note their existence in passing.

The Hon. Murray Finch-Hatton, Member for the Sleaford Division, writes:—

'Allotments are of two kinds—arable and pasture.

'1. *Arable.*—I give each labourer as much arable land as he can work in his spare time. This will be about one rood if he has a fair garden with his house besides, and perhaps half an acre if he has not. Much will depend upon his family and the help they are of an age to render him. The conditions necessary for success are (1) fairly good land; (2) a fair rent; (3) distance not more than half a mile from his house, nearer, of course, if possible; (4) access by cartway to a good road; (5) the number of allotments to be carefully proportioned to the number of labourers likely to want them, so as to create a little competition for them and keep cultivation up to the mark.

'2. *Grass*, which is deserving, perhaps, of a somewhat different name, and vary in different cases from one cow's grass up to the dimensions of a tiny grass or dairy farm. The rule here is to give a labourer as much grass land with his cottage as he has money to stock. The cottage themselves selected for such tenancies should be good, substantial ones, with a small cool room for a dairy, either inside the house or not, and a shed or hovel for the stock. With us they are known as " cow cottages," and are always in request.

'It often happens that a labourer, while in service and before he marries, is able to save a fair sum of money, and the knowledge that such a cottage may present itself to him as a means of investing it to advantage is a powerful inducement to many to do so ; the advantage here again, as in the last case, is that an addition to income may be made without loss of wages.

'The wife looks after the stock, milks the cow, and attends to the dairy, while the husband works on the neighbouring farm at daily wages—indeed four or five of the best workmen I have on my own farm are tenants of this kind. They pay their rents with the greatest regularity, and even in these bad times have asked for no substantial reduction of them ; on the contrary, if any grass land near the village becomes vacant, they are usually applicants for it, which means that they have in the meantime made such an addition to their capital, or, what is the same thing, to their stock, as will justify them in increasing their occupation. Sometimes, where a field is too large for one such tenant, I let it to three conjointly, each of whom has the right to pasture a certain quantity of stock, and I have lately sanctioned, on an estate in Northants, for the owners of which I act, an arrangement by which the whole occupation of a retiring grazier is let to ten applicants from the neighbouring village conjointly as a cow common.'

I have already had occasion to speak of the Saffron Walden experiment in Essex. In the same neighbourgood an inquiry recently made revealed the fact that in twenty-three parishes, embracing an area of nearly 64,000 acres, there are 223 acres of land laid out in upwards of 1,300 allotments of from one-sixth of an acre to half an acre each, and let (except in some few exceptional cases, where the plots partake more of the nature of gardens than allotments) at from $1\frac{1}{2}d$. to $4\frac{1}{2}d$. per rod; the rates and tithe, as well as the cost of maintaining the fences, &c., being in every instance paid by the owners of the land. In eighteen of the twenty-three parishes visited (embracing an area of about 41,000 acres), nearly all the occupiers of land allow their labourers to grow from ten to forty rods of potatoes on their farms every year, without charging them any rent for the ground, the usual conditions being that the men find a load of manure for every ten rods and keep the crop clean; the employer carting the manure, doing all necessary operations of tillage, and carting the crop home for them. In some cases this privilege is extended to widows of deceased labourers; and in a few instances the farmers themselves provide the manure without charge.

More than thirty years ago, Mr. (now Sir John) Lawes
set apart from eight to ten acres, and a few years later
about an equal area, so that for more than twenty-five
years there have been between sixteen and seventeen
acres let in allotments, for the most part of one-eighth
of an acre each, a few somewhat less, the whole
number of tenants being 171. The land actually
occupied was let at 40s. an acre; but, as besides
this, nearly two acres were laid out in roads, at the
cost of the landlord, and this pays no rent, the return
per acre on the whole area devoted is much less. The
landlord, moreover, keeps the roads in order, and
has built and maintains a club-house for the tenants,
so that, in fact, the return on the whole transaction is
merely nominal, if indeed there be not a loss.

So great has been the boon that there have always
been more candidates for plots than vacancies, and in
1883 rather more than nine acres more were allotted to
seventy-eight tenants at the same rate per acre of the
actually occupied land; but here, again, land was
sacrificed for roads made by the landlord and paying
no rent. Most of these allotments were like the
others—one-eighth of an acre each—but some rather
less, the whole averaging about one-ninth of an acre.
It is the unwritten law that the above allotments
should be devoted to garden (not agricultural) crops
for the benefit of the families of the holders; and experience has amply shown that, for this purpose, one-

E

eighth of an acre is quite as much as a man with other occupations can work; whilst, if properly worked, it will produce quite as much garden crops as will be required by an average-sized family. Indeed, those with small families find it ·more than they want, and sometimes have produce to sell, though with so many gardens in the neighbourhood there is only a restricted market.

So much for mere garden allotments. But for some time past Sir John has wished to try how far it would be beneficial to grant larger areas. Accordingly he has, this Michaelmas (1885), set apart two fields, close to a large hamlet of the parish, comprising rather over twenty acres, to be let in larger allotments if desired, and the land has been taken up as follows :—

> 23 one-eighth acre each.
> 7 one-fourth   ,,
> 3 half   ,,
> 11 one   ,,
> 2 rather under one acre.
> 1 ,,   over   ,,
> ――
> 47

It will be seen that still the larger number take up only one-eighth or one-quarter of an acre. Of the three with half an acre each, two are farm labourers and one a butcher. Of the fourteen with larger areas only six are farm labourers, the remainder being butchers, jobbing carters, blacksmiths, or carpenters, &c.

Already one lot of six, and another of three, are considering whether they cannot work their plots together. Some of the labourers are not in full employment, and so hope to utilise their spare time. Some of the other people have horses, or ponies, or other live stock, so that to them the plots will probably be profitable. It remains to be seen what will be the success of these larger holdings in other cases.

In connection with these allotments Sir John has started an 'Allotment Club.' To become a member of the club, it is necessary to possess an allotment-garden, the ordinary size of which is one-eighth of an acre, and the rent 5s. per annum, although some allotments are only half that size. Sir John occasionally gives prizes for the best cultivated gardens, and every second year there is a show of vegetables. The men take immense interest in these gardens.

At the annual dinner, which takes place the first Saturday in June, Sir John has an opportunity of meeting almost all the members of the club, and of discussing subjects of mutual interest; even the delicate one of 'strikes' has not been avoided, and a discussion on the subject, bearing upon the relation between the employers of labour and the labourers, has not in any way altered the friendly feeling between them. The influence of the club upon the moral and religious condition of the members can hardly be discussed in these pages. Anyone, however, who reads over the rules of the club, published in the Appendix, and considers that they have been formed by a committee elected by the annual vote of every member of the club, and that they are not merely printed rules, but are rigidly enforced, must acknowledge that the members submitting to these rules must have arrived at a position considerably in advance of that generally accorded to the agricultural labourer in this country.

In Suffolk, the greatest pains have been taken on the estates of Sir E. Kerrison and Lord Henniker to give to the labourer an opportunity of having an interest in the cultivation of the soil. On Sir Edward's there are over 500 allotments now, although about four years ago, when the severity of the bad seasons and prices were beginning to be felt, it was found necessary to plough up ten acres of the allotment land for want of tenants.

Lord Henniker makes a practice of watching carefully the progress made by allotment tenants, and where a man shows that he has saved a sufficient sum to stock more land, and has the energy and ability to cultivate a larger space, Lord Henniker allows him gradually to increase the size of his holding.

The Duke of Grafton's allotments, of which there are 820, are let at a rent of 29s. an acre, as compared with 25s. charged for adjoining land let in farms. The

Duke gives every facility for the holding of allotments by his labourers.

Lord Bristol has issued a circular to all labourers residing in parishes where he owns land, offering to let them allotments. It will be interesting to know the result of this experiment.

In Norfolk the allotment system is very generally in force, though it is probable that in this, as in the adjoining county of Suffolk, where the facilities given by the Allotments Act, 1882, have been largely made use of, more allotments could readily be let. In 1835 Lord Suffield, charging the grand jury of the county, expressed it as his conviction that the only method of improving the condition of the agricultural labourer which was free from objection, was that of providing him with a small area of land to cultivate. The Earl of Kimberley has let allotments for over forty years on his Norfolk estate, but Colonel Bulwer has offered to cut up forty acres in one parish in Norfolk without having had a single response.

On H.R.H. the Prince of Wales's Sandringham estate the men are reported not to care for allotments, though some have them at Dersingham and in two other villages. Mr. Beck says: 'In Sandringham they are not much thought about. A man has a nice house and garden, his constant work, and goes to it, and does not really care for an allotment.'

In Wales, where there are so many small holdings, allotments proper are hardly known.

Lord Sudeley, writing of his Welsh property, says:
'On the Gregynog Estate the proportion of small farms
is fully maintained, and there are at present no less
than seventy-six small holdings under forty-five acres,
and that of those fifty range from two to eleven acres,
so that ample scope is given to the smaller tenantry to
gradually rise to larger-sized farms. This principle of
granting in arable districts quarter or half an acre, or
instead, where there is pasture available, land under
proper conditions sufficient to enable cottagers to keep
a cow, is one which I have always been much in favour
of, and I am extremely glad to see that there is a wish
to have this system more fully carried out. It is not, of
course, possible in every case to give sufficient pasture
to keep a cow, as due regard must be paid to the conditions and requirements of the neighbouring farms,
but, so far as I am concerned, I can only say that I
should be extremely pleased to see no exception to the
rule, and that in all cases where it is wished industrious
and thrifty persons in cottages on the Gregynog Estate
should be possessed either of half an acre of garden-
land, or, where possible in pasture districts and where
the tenant has sufficient capital, land enough to keep
a cow. It will be clearly quite impossible to extend
this system hurriedly, but every consideration will
be given to carry it out fully as soon as possible.
Arrangements have been made with some of the
farmers to give up a few of their fields near the prin-

cipal village on the estate. This district is mainly
pasture, and allotments of this class of land are
being made to some eight cottagers. As, however, on
the Welsh estate there is such a large proportion of
small holdings, very little is found to be necessary.

On Lord Sudeley's estate at Toddington, in
Gloucestershire, where a large portion of the land is
arable, the cottagers are allowed to have an extra
quarter-acre, making up half an acre if desired; but
only in two or three instances has any request been
made to carry this out, and quarter-acre gardens are
considered, save in exceptional circumstances, to be
quite sufficient.

I have not entered into the question of allotments in Scotland for several reasons—first, because I
have no special knowledge of the agricultural parts of
that country; secondly, because Sir Edward Colebrook,
in his 'Small Holdings,' has collected all the information existing on the point; and, thirdly, because I have
yet to learn that there is any demand for them in
Scotland. In the south-eastern counties the former
practice of grazing the labourer's cow along with those
of the farmer, his employer, has given place to the
simpler practice of giving to him a daily supply of
milk from the farmer's dairy, and in many parts this
is supplemented by a specified quantity of barley and
oats for grinding, to which is added the use of ground
for a certain number of drills of potatoes, the farm
servant supplying the seed and labour.

HOW TO SET OUT ALLOTMENTS.

THE facts referred to in the preceding chapter show how much has already been done in the direction of letting land to the labourer.

It remains now to be seen how far there exists a desire on the part of the labourer for further facilities in this direction. It is most unfortunate that we should have no recent return of the number of allotments in the country. Mr. Morton, in his 'Encyclopædia of Agriculture,' published in 1855, estimates the number of allotments at 200,000.

The agricultural returns for 1870 contained a return of all holdings under five acres. That return being a tentative one, was incomplete.

The total for England was—holdings not exceeding five acres, 102,342; from five to twenty acres, 111,284. Of the five-acre holdings, 49,000, or about two-thirds, were held as allotments by agricultural labourers and working men.

It was succeeded in 1872 by a more comprehensive return—of holdings of one-fourth of an acre, and of holdings from one to five acres.

The return of 1872 was also admitted to be defective, partly because land sublet in allotments had been returned in the aggregate by the persons subletting, and partly because some of the collecting officers left out of the return holdings which had not a crop amounting to one quarter of an acre. It was also defective on account of so many allotments being one-eighth of an acre and under.

In 1873 the inquiry as to allotments was renewed, ' and made, as far as practicable, to extend to all garden allotments detached from the houses of agricultural labourers and artisans.' The return for that year showed a total of 246,000 such allotments, of which 242,000 were in England.

In that year the number of agricultural labourers, farm servants, and cottagers was estimated at 764,928, which of course include the migratory population of the North, for whom it has been shown allotments have no attractions; but even taking these imperfect returns, we have more than one allotment for every three labourers, besides any advantage which may be derived from the garden attached to his cottage, all of which were excluded from the statistics collected by the Agricultural Department. Since 1873 no similar returns have been published.

It is difficult, in the face of these facts, to believe that there is any real indisposition on the part of landowners to grant allotments; that which is far more probable is, that there has been a reluctance on the part of labourers to ask for the accommodation.

I am far from desiring to detract from the service which Mr. Chamberlain and others have rendered to the agricultural labourer by stimulating him to give expression to his wishes, and by calling the attention of landowners to the desire which exists in the mind of the labourer to possess an allotment. The latter, however, is not yet sufficiently advanced to dispense with some guiding hand, and it is well that those who have at command the results of the experience of others should point out to him that the area which he can profitably cultivate must necessarily be limited by the energy he displays, the assistance he can command from members of his family, and the funds at his disposal wherewith to stock it. Nothing could be more inimical to the interests of the labourer than to endeavour to persuade him that, because he has successfully and profitably cultivated a quarter or half an acre in his spare time, he can with advantage sacrifice some of his wage-earning hours to bestow on his allotment. The 13s. to 15s. a week which a labourer may earn ought on no account to be endangered, but the allotment in all cases should be looked upon as the recreation of leisure time.

These remarks do not, of course, apply to pasture allotments, where the wife may be able to do almost

all the dairy-work, and it will only be in time of hay har-
vest that any serious call will be made on the time of the
labourer. It must not therefore be supposed that
labourers or their wives in every part of England are
competent to manage a dairy allotment; in most of the
merely arable counties dairying is entirely unknown,
and a cow would be a perfect white elephant.

It would be a most interesting experiment if
some landowners would endeavour to procure the
education of farm labourers' wives and daughters to
dairy-work with a view to establishing the system on
their estates; it is not improbable that the cottagers
would quickly learn of each other, and in a country
where grass was available this might easily be done.
The expense of erecting cow-byres should not be heavy
if constructed of materials on the estate, and their cost
would soon be recovered out of the rental.

Much depends on the situation of the allotment.
The best of all is where each cottage has its allotment adjoining. Lord Tollemache's are thus arranged;
a result which he has attained in many cases by
straightening the boundary of a field, so rendering
it of more useful shape for steam cultivation, and
the oddment cut off has been utilised as a cottage
allotment. Where cottages are already built, and
especially in villages, this practice is not possible, and
the next best course is to devote to the purpose a
centrally situated field adjoining the high road, and

easily reached by carts, &c. In no case should the allotment be more than half a mile from the labourer's dwelling.

The landlord should pay all rates, taxes, and outgoings whatsoever, keep the gates, fences, and all but the boundaries between the allotments, in repair himself.

Where cow 'gaits' cannot be given, two pasture fields, of which one can be grazed and the other mown for hay, to be held in common by labourers, is an excellent and highly appreciated plan of providing an allotment. Wherever possible the labourer should be allowed to keep a pig; the manure is of the greatest benefit to the allotment. Lord Winchelsea reckoned that fifty perches of land would keep an average family in vegetables, and besides supply sufficient for the keep of a pig, rabbits, fowls, or ducks.

The rent is an important point, and one in which the greatest care should be exercised. It is well known that labourers can, and will, pay a very high rent for allotment land, but it is in the last degree unwise to insist on a rent higher than the same land would command if devoted to other purposes.

In cases where the land is near a town, and is in the nature of accommodation land, a somewhat higher rent may be demanded, but in agricultural districts not a penny more should be asked than would be received for the same land if let in a farm, after adding the cost of all outgoings, repairs, collection, and, if the receipt of rent is doubtful, a small percentage for bad debts.

As it is unadvisable to demand a high rent, so is it equally undesirable to let land free or below its value. The labourer rarely values that for which he pays nothing, and if his tenure has in it anything of an eleemosynary character he will never be sure that his landlord may not withdraw his favour and dispossess him of the land.

This should never be done except the land be wanted for building or some public purpose. In every such case there should be a clause binding the landlord to make the fullest compensation, such as a tenant would expect if compulsorily expropriated for a railway or other work of a public nature.

Of course such a provision would not apply to cases of forfeiture for non-payment of rent or conviction of crime, nor for a breach of the rules or agreement; even in these cases the tenant should not be dispossessed of his crops without compensation. Captain Scobell says ' the effect of this guarantee will astonish you, even in the worst characters before.'

As to the persons who should hold allotments, if proper provisions for payment of rent, &c. be made, no landlord should be afraid of accepting as tenant a man of idle or dissolute habits; it may be the salvation of him, and the necessity of complying with the rules will keep the allotment in a fair state of cultivation.

In some cases there is a provision for the election of a jury of allotment-holders, to decide upon the amount to be paid between an incoming and outgoing tenant.

Here are Captain Scobell's recommendations:— ' The regulations I would recommend, from experience, are these, and which I have never known to fail, although applied in very many parishes under different circumstances. Announce your intention of letting field gardens in your parish, ascertain the number of labourers, the size of each family, and the quantity of garden ground then in occupation of each. Exclude none for previous bad character; they may be reclaimed. Do not include any paupers. *Let no parish officers have anything to do with the arrangements.* If your population is scattered, fix on two or more fields rather than one large one. The quality of the land should be good and fresh, the quantity to each family from ten to fifty poles. If a man occupies more than he can permanently uphold by manure, the land will be losing stamina. Divide the field into strips, from top to bottom, abutting against the highway. All manure should be carted in the winter months, when it can be done without injury. Let the parties who are to have the same sized gardens draw lots. Have no favourites; the fields should be as near as practicable and easy of access, the hedges should be cut low, and kept so, and an additional gate or stile added. The rules should be few and clear, and each have a copy. Whatever charges besides rent are made, such as tithes and rates, should be distinguished from the rent itself; the whole year's rent should be made at one payment, in the autumn. Condition, not to dispossess your tenants, except on conviction, by law, of some crime or wilful breach of the regulations. If you give any awards for good cultivation, let it be in tools or seeds, or clothes, and not in money. There should be a condition that, if any tenant subjects himself to removal, he will surrender up his occupation on being required so to do. Have no fear of the trouble, it will be a light amusement. If you cross the fields but twice in the year, and see your tenantry once in the year assembled together, the system will work quietly and well.'

VOLUNTARY VERSUS *COMPULSORY* *ALLOTMENTS.*

I DO not purpose to enter into my own views as to whether it is desirable, in order to extend not only the system of allotments, but also that of small holdings, to have recourse to compulsory legislation. I think that the opinion of authorities whose names are well known as upholders of the allotment system is likely to have far greater weight with my readers than my own.

There is first Lord Tollemache, who has been accepted by the introducers of the Small Holdings Bill as the model landlord of England, and whose opinion they give as follows: 'Railway directors and dock trustees are given compulsory powers for the purchase of land to enable them to carry out their undertakings for the benefit of the public, and for this reason local authorities might be given the same for promoting the comfort and welfare of the middle and labouring classes in the district.' But this does not by any means fairly represent the whole case with regard to Lord Tollemache's opinion. The 'Times' published a letter from his lordship, dated September 12, 1885, in which he says: '*By*

far the most effectual and satisfactory way of extending
this system is by the voluntary action of the landlords ;
but if no decided movement takes place on their part
in the matter, as a last resource, not only for the comfort and advantage of the middle and labouring classes,
but for the protection of the just rights of landed property generally, the compulsory powers you allude to
ought, in my opinion, to be adopted, accompanied by
conditions, such as an ample notice being given to the
owners of land, e.g. a year's notice to be given to landed
proprietors to enable them to commence carrying out
the system of granting allotments to labourers and
small holdings to middle-class people, so that compulsory powers will not be applicable to their estates, with
powers of appeal, &c. . . . I still hope that compulsory powers will be altogether avoided.'

Writing of a Shropshire proprietor, whose estàte he
visited, Mr. Impey says : ' Colonel Edwards, describing
his own village, made use of the words, " It is a village
where there is no poverty," giving this as the completest
justification of his adherence to the system of labourers'
small holdings.' And again, he says Colonel Edwards'
decision as to the system of management adopted
on his property 'will certainly strengthen the hands
of those who are urging its adoption on public grounds.

But let us see what Colonel Edwards himself says
upon this point. Writing to Mr. Impey on January 28
last, he says :—

'It is improbable we shall ever agree on the steps
to be taken to insure the increase in the number of
small holdings; you want to do it by coercion, I want
to do it by example and persuasion. You allow my
estate, a very small one, to be almost a perfect pattern.
Your measures would tend to rob and ruin me. To
many large farmers some of my ideas are, I fear, very
unpopular, and as soon as irresponsible County Boards,
with powers to take land compulsorily, are created, I
and people like myself would be the first to suffer and
to have land stolen from us. No labourer could live on
three acres of land without regular employment, and
there would be no employment for more labourers here.
I have formerly worked at field labour voluntarily with
the people, ploughing and harvesting, and have the
experience of a very long life, being far on in my
seventy-sixth year, but *I would resist your plunder,
even if legalised, to the death.*'

Colonel Edwards says that one of the labourers,
whose holding on his estate is so graphically described
by Mr. Impey in 'Three Acres and a Cow,' being
asked whether ownerships of small holdings would
answer, at once said, 'No, it would not pay to buy,
as no funds would be put by for repairs, the places
would soon be dilapidated, and the people and children
would all become *bellyproud*, and soon ruin themselves.'

Colonel Edwards adds: 'Several instances of the

above have come under their own knowledge as well as mine, and small places are now mortgaged beyond their value. I am sure that, where labourers are steady, and have wives who are good managers, and who are able to milk and manage their little dairy, a few acres of grass land adjoining their cottages are of great assistance to them ; but it is not *all* cottagers who are fit to have land, and the fitness must be determined by the owner who lets the land. A few years ago a carpenter in this neighbourhood married the upper housemaid from my family. She was a very tidy, respectable servant, and was the daughter of my old gardener, who has about four acres of land with his cottage. Two years after her marriage one of my cottages, with about five acres of land, became vacant, and I allowed them to rent it. They were unable to carry it on. She, though a very good servant, could not manage a cow, and in seven years' time they were obliged to leave and go into a cottage with only a garden, and have since got on much better. I mention this case to show that compulsory allotments will not answer. Everybody is inclined to cry out for what they see others benefiting by, never considering whether they are capable of doing likewise.'

Mr. Goschen, an active supporter of the Land and Glebe Owners' Association for the Voluntary Extension of the Allotments System, said, in his speech on Mr. Collings' motion, on January 26: 'I say it is a

'dangerous experiment, because while you are trying
'your experiment you may discourage that voluntary
'movement which is at present going on. A good many
'landlords who are prepared now with allotments might
'much prefer that they should sell their land to the
'community, and that then the community should take
'all the disagreeable labour of collecting the rents from
'the tenants of all these small allotments. I think you
'will remove a great part of the duty from the landlords,
'and you will remove that to which I attach the greatest
'importance—the sense of duty on the part of the land-
'lords that they ought to give these allotments. If
'the State, the community, comes in and says, "On us
'"rests the responsibility of carrying out this move-
'" ment," will you not discourage the other class? Well,
'that is a matter of opinion only, hon. members will
'say. But I am bound, conscientiously believing that
'it will discourage the sense of duty on the part of the
'landlords, to express this opinion to the House.'

Dr. Gilbert, writing a report on Sir John Lawes'
allotments to Sir Lyon Playfair, says: 'There can be
little doubt that where proximity to the dwellings
renders it practicable, garden allotments are a very
great boon. Further, market gardening, and the production of milk and poultry on comparatively small
holdings, might with advantage be extended in suitable
localities. But the idea that what are called small
farms, with or without proprietorship, and with re-

stricted or borrowed working capital, can compete in
general agriculture with moderately sized ones, large
enough to take advantage of machinery and other
improved methods for economical production, in these
days of active foreign competition, is, I believe, quite
chimerical, and its advocacy very mischievous.'

Even Mr. Impey in his work admits that in many
cases the extension of the system could best be done
by the landlords.

There can be no doubt that the extent to which
the allotment system has been carried out is little
realised. The present, the writer believes, is the first
attempt that has been made to trace in detail its
development throughout the country; and the result
is to show that land for allotments and small holdings
is at the disposal of labourers in all quarters of
England, that it has been so for many years past, that
the offer is not made grudgingly, but that they are
cordially invited to occupy plots of varying dimensions,
according to the quantity which they believe they can
cultivate or turn to account.

The facts and figures which are given in this book
must surely be accepted as disproving a charge which
has been brought against landowners, to the effect that
they have no consideration for the well-being of their
humble neighbours who till the ground. It will be
seen that the granting of plots of land, on easy terms,
to those who desire them, is now the general custom,

and has been so in a greater or less degree for many years past. The demand has lately become greater, and the large and exceedingly influential list of members of the Association given in this book abundantly shows that these demands will not be made in vain. It has been my object to avoid polemics, to make no assertions as to ignorance—malicious, culpable, or excusable—on the part of those who cry out that the labourer's well-being is a matter of no concern to landowners, and that only by compulsion can he obtain such help and assistance as an allotment may bring. I have endeavoured simply to give a plain account of the true state of the case as it exists, and of its prospects of extension.

Two points remain for comment.

Colonel Edwards is, as aforesaid, held up by Mr. Impey as a model landlord; and it will be seen above how he regards the threat of compulsion. Many owners of property think with him; and without laying stress on the numerous kindly services which a landlord can, and in so very many cases gladly does, perform for a welcome tenant, or on the other hand making capital of the ill-feeling and trouble which would spring up from the quartering on a property of unwelcome settlers, the second point arises: whether the labourer himself would prefer the voluntary or the compulsory system? It is professedly on behalf of the labourers that the compulsionists agitate, and the labourers must therefore be

regarded.   We have yet to learn of any meeting of
labourers asking for allotments which they cannot obtain, nor shall we hear of such a grievance, for, let it
be repeated, allotments are now, under existing conditions, within the reach of all who care for them ;
in certain places and under certain circumstances they
are a boon, in other places they are a profitless responsibility.

In those districts where labourers do desire land, I
myself have no doubt as to what their emphatic choice
would be, between a holding obtained under a compulsory enactment and one freely granted from a
member of the Association on behalf of which this
little volume is issued.

APPENDIX.

RULES AND REGULATIONS OF THE ROTHAMSTED ALLOTMENT CLUB.

1. Everyone elected as a member shall pay one shilling entrance fee; he shall sign his name to the rules, and shall pay one halfpenny weekly to the club, and threepence on the death of any member or his wife.

2. Any person wishing to take an allotment garden can have his name written on a board, to be hung up in the club-room, in the following form :—A. B. proposed by C. D., member.

3. When a vacancy occurs in an allotment garden, the names of the candidates shall be taken in the order they are written on the board, and they shall be voted on at a meeting of the committee.

4. The club shall be managed by a committee of twelve members, who shall hold office for one year; they shall have power to make rules, and the whole management of the club shall be in their hands.

5. The annual meeting of the club shall take place in the month of June, on which occasion the committee for the succeeding year shall be elected. The members of the committee may be re-elected, but it shall be competent for any member of the club to nominate any other member to serve on the committee. The election to be decided by a majority of votes.

6. Each member to draw the beer in order, according to the number of his allotment; on failing to do so, a forfeit of one penny to be paid to the club.

7. The member who draws the beer shall be in attendance at the club-room every week-day at six o'clock : if he is not there at a quarter-past six, he shall be fined threepence ; if he does not attend at all he shall be fined sixpence. He is to remain until ten o'clock, but in the event of no member being present at nine o'clock, he may shut up the room at that hour.

8. The member whose turn it is to draw the beer shall receive from the previous member the oath-book, sixteen shillings and sixpence, and half a barrel of beer, and shall deliver over these articles to the succeeding member. He shall also pay over to the brewer the sum of sixteen shillings and sixpence, and order half a barrel of beer. Any neglect of this rule shall make him liable to a penalty of five shillings, for which sum he shall be sued in the County Court, as well as for any deficiency in the amount of money entrusted to him.

9. Any member selling beer shall be expelled from the club.

10. Any member giving beer to anyone except to his wife and children, or to his brother and sister, will be fined one shilling.

11. Any member drawing beer on a Sunday morning shall be liable to a penalty of one shilling, to be paid to the club.

12. Any member drawing beer after ten o'clock, except on a quarter night, when half an hour longer will be allowed, shall be liable to a penalty of sixpence, to be paid to the club.

13. Any member making, or causing others to make, any disturbance or row in the club-room, will be fined threepence.

14. Any member swearing, or repeating an oath in the

club-room, or under the verandah outside the door, shall be liable to a penalty of twopence each time, to be paid to the club.

15. Any member getting vegetables in the garden-fields after nine o'clock on a Sunday morning, by Rothamsted time, will be fined sixpence.

16. Any member not paying his money before ten o'clock on the quarter night will be fined threepence; if not paid within one month from that date, he will cease to be a member of the club, and will forfeit his garden; he can then only enter the club by a fresh election and the payment of a fine of one shilling.

17. Any member not keeping his allotment-garden clear from seed-weeds, or otherwise injuring his neighbours, may be turned out of his garden by the votes of two-thirds of the committee, after receiving proper notice.

18. Any member wishing to give up his allotment must give notice to the committee, and the succeeding tenant can enter on any part of the allotment which is uncropped at the time of notice of the leaving tenant.

19. The committee shall meet four times every year for transacting the business of the club, namely, on the first Monday in January, the first Monday in April, the first Monday in July, and the first Monday in October, from seven to eight o'clock in the evening. Any member not attending, except in the event of illness, shall pay threepence to the funds; and no member shall allow his name to be put down to serve on the committee unless he is in a position to attend and take an interest in the same.

20. As soon as possible after the death of a member of the club, the sum of 2l. shall be paid out of the funds of the club to the widow, or widower, or if the member is not married, to the nearest relation.

21. Any member drawing or giving beer to those who are expelled from the club shall be fined threepence.

22. No member shall be entitled to the money paid at death until he has paid up all his subscriptions and fines for twelve months.

23. Any member breaking a mug is to pay the cost of replacing the same.

24. Rents for the gardens are due on the 29th of September; if not paid within one month of that date, the members who have not paid will forfeit their allotments, and will be proceeded against by the committee for the amount due in the County Court. If paid between the 29th of September and the 29th of October, a fine of sixpence will have to be paid.

25. Any member or members belonging to this society found fighting, or striking in the room or in the field, will be liable to a penalty of five shillings for each offence, to be paid to the club.

26. The books of this society shall be examined every half-year, and a full statement made of the income and expenditure of the society at a general meeting, and a full report shall be presented to the members at the annual meeting of the members in June.

27. Any member taking tools from another man's garden without leave, and not returning them the same day, will be fined one shilling.

28. Any member laying dung on the gravel roads will be fined one shilling for the first offence, and for the second offence he will be expelled from the club.

29. Any member who sells the produce of his garden to a stranger must be present himself—or some of his family must be present, or he must give notice to the man who attends to the walks to be present—when the produce is cut or removed. If the purchaser removes the produce without a witness, the owner of the garden will be fined one shilling.

30. When a member has drawn his barrel of beer, he must show himself in the club-room, and ask for the next

member to take his place, or be fined one shilling; but if no one is there to take it, he can tap a second barrel.

31. Any member making a dispute about any of the rules, it shall be settled by the committee, and their decision shall be final.

Model Form of Agreement.

A. B., of   , Esquire (the landlord), hereby agrees to let, and C. D., of   aforesaid, labourer (the tenant), hereby agrees to take the allotment of land situate at   aforesaid, numbered   on the plan of the landlord's field garden allotments, and containing   poles or thereabouts, from September 29, 188   , from year to year at the yearly rent of   , payable weekly after notice to that effect (yet so that no arrears be made payable by such notice) but otherwise on September 29 in each year free of all rates, taxes, and tithe rent-charge, all of which will be paid by the landlord. The landlord and the tenant respectively agree to abide by and carry out the rules above written, and the tenant agrees to hold his allotment subject to such rules as though they were embodied in this agreement.

Dated September 29, 188
    Witness

```
Stamp

6d.
```

Note.—The original agreement with the rules at the head should be signed by the landlord, and a counterpart by the tenant. The two should then be exchanged, and the original should be kept by the tenant and the counterpart by the landlord.

The agreement is subject to a stamp duty of 6*d*.   This may be denoted by an adhesive Postage and Inland Revenue Stamp, which must be cancelled by the person by whom the agreement is first executed, who should write his name or initials and the date across the stamp.

The stamp should be on the original, signed by the landlord, and the counterpart need not be stamped (Stamp Act, 1870, ss. 36 & 93).

RULES OF THE FIELD GARDEN ALLOTMENTS AT X,
IN THE COUNTY OF Y.

1. The tenant shall not underlet or part with the possession of his allotment or any part of it.

2. The tenant shall cultivate his allotment by spade husbandry only, and shall keep it clean, well manured, and properly cultivated and cropped as a field garden.   He shall not work upon his allotment on Sunday, nor erect any building thereon, nor grow white straw crops on the same part of his allotment two years in succession.   The tenant may, by special permission in writing given by the landlord or his agent, be allowed to cultivate or crop his allotment otherwise than as above stated ; and permission will usually be given to erect a pigsty, on condition that all the manure therefrom shall be applied to the allotment.

3. At the end or determination of the tenancy, the tenant shall peaceably quit and deliver up possession of the allotment and everything growing or fixed thereon to the landlord or to whom he shall appoint.

4. The tenant shall not throw or leave any manure, soil, stones, weeds, or rubbish on to any path or road, or into any ditch, stream, well, or pond or otherwise obstruct the same,

and shall keep the drains and paths under, on, or adjoining his allotment clean and in proper order, and shall not remove, damage, foul, or misuse the fences, walls, baulks, gates, stiles, trees, ditches, drains, pumps, ponds, wells, watercourses, paths, or roads of, or adjoining, the allotment field, or the stumps marking the boundaries or the numbers of the different allotments, but, on the contrary, shall protect and preserve the same to the best of his power.

5. The tenant shall not encroach, trespass, or commit any depredation or damage on the other allotments or on the land of the landlord, and agrees so to manage and use his allotment, and so to behave himself while in the allotment field as not to cause any nuisance or annoyance to the other tenants, or to the landlord, and to assist and give evidence in order to discover and convict persons who so offend.

6. Either landlord or tenant may put an end to the tenancy on September 29, in the first or any other year, by giving to the other of them six calendar months' previous notice in writing.

7. Every notice to the landlord may be served on him by giving it to his agent, to whom also rent may be paid, and every notice to the tenant may be served on him either personally or by leaving it at his last known place of abode, or on any part of his allotment.

8. The tenant shall be entitled, on quitting his holding at the end of his tenancy, to obtain from the landlord, as compensation for the growing crops, fruit trees and bushes, and for unexhausted manure and labour, such sum as fairly represents the value thereof to an incoming tenant, less any sums due for rent or assessed as damages for waste or breach of this agreement. All such sums shall be assessed by the landlord's agent, whose decision shall be final, unless the tenant, within ten days after notice of such decision, give notice in writing that he requires such sums to be assessed by a reference as under the Agricultural Holdings (England) Act, 1883, so far as regards procedure, and gives sufficient

security for the costs of such reference, provided that no compensation shall be payable to the tenant unless claimed by notice in writing delivered four weeks before the expiration of the tenancy.

9. If any rent shall be in arrear for ten days, whether legally demanded or not, or if the tenant wilfully break any of the above conditions, or if he be convicted of any offence whereby he shall be liable to fine or imprisonment, or if he cease to reside in the parish, or within two miles from his allotment without giving previous notice in writing to the landlord of some address where he can be found, it shall be lawful for the landlord to re-enter and take possession of the allotment and every crop and other thing thereon, and thereupon the tenancy shall be determined. The tenant may by notice in writing, delivered to the landlord within ten days after such re-entry, claim compensation, and if so claimed, compensation shall be assessed in manner aforesaid, except that the decision of the landlord's agent shall in all cases be final, and the sum (if any) assessed as compensation shall be paid to or applied for the benefit of the tenant, his wife, children, parents, creditors, or any of them in such manner as the landlord or his agent shall think fit.

10. The death of the tenant shall of itself put an end to the tenancy, and thereupon compensation shall be assessed and paid or applied in the same manner as last mentioned, without any claim being made by any person.

11. The landlord agrees not to give notice to quit unless the rent is in arrear, or unless the tenant shall have broken any of the above conditions or shall have applied for relief at the expense of the poor-rate (except medical relief) for himself or any member of his family, or shall cease to reside in the parish or within one mile from his allotment, or shall have been convicted of any offence whereby he shall be liable to fine or imprisonment, or unless the allotment or any part of it is required for any purpose inconsistent with the use of the land as allotment or market garden or farm land.

RULES OF THE HAINTON ESTATE COW CLUB.

1.—That a Cow Club be formed for the parishes of Hainton, South Willingham, Benniworth, Sixhills, Legsby, East Barkwith, and East Torrington, and be called the "Hainton Estate Cow Club."

2.—That the "Hainton Estate Cow Club" do consist of a President, Treasurer, Committee, and other subscription members.

3.—That the Committee consist of three members from each of the parishes of South Willingham and Benniworth, and two each from the parishes of Hainton and Sixhills, in addition to the President and Treasurer, who shall be ex-officio members of the Committee, all of whom (except the President) shall retire at the annual general meeting of the Club in April, but be eligible for re-election.

4.—That persons eligible to become members of the Club be tenants on the Hainton Estate paying less than fifty pounds a year rent, or such other cottagers in those parishes as the Committee may consider it desirable to admit.

5.—That the accounts of the Club be balanced on the 31st day of March in each year, and duly audited and examined by the Auditor of the Club (who shall be appointed by the Committee) and presented at the general meeting.

6.—That a general meeting of the Club be held on some convenient day (to be fixed by the Committee) within the first fortnight of April.

7.—That each member pay five shillings for each cow entered, and a fee of two shillings and sixpence for every change of cow, and that the subscription be one shilling per month, and paid monthly to the person appointed to receive the same in each district, and shall be paid on the first Monday in each month.

8.—That the Committee shall appoint one of their number in each district to receive members' subscriptions, who shall

G

transmit them before the end of the first whole week in each month to the Treasurer, who shall deposit the same in the Post Office Savings Bank before the last day of the same month.

9.—That any member neglecting to pay his subscriptions for three months in succession shall be warned thereof by the receiver of subscriptions in his district, and if he does not pay up the arrears on the first Monday of the following month he shall cease to be a member of the Club.

10.—That anyone desirous of entering a cow shall give notice to the members of the Committee in his district, who shall examine into the age, health, and value of the cow proposed to be entered.

11.—That no cow be entered in the Club above the age of seven years, nor of the less yearly average value than twelve pounds.

12.—That no member can receive any benefit from the fund whose cow dies of milk fever or lung complaint, if it can be shown that to the owner's knowledge the said cow has had the disease before.

13.—That a marking pincers be provided for the Club for the purpose of marking the cow entered.

14.—That each cow passed by the Committee shall be marked on the ear on the milking side with the Club marker, and no cow shall be deemed duly entered until so marked.

15.—That when any cow is taken ill the owner shall apply to the person who keeps the drinks in his district, who shall go and see the cow, and, if he thinks it necessary, shall direct the owner to call in the farrier without loss of time.

16.—That in case of sudden emergency it shall be in the power of the Committee to allow the owner the cost of any necessary medicine administered, though the Club farrier had not been called in.

17.—That any member of this society losing a cow be allowed from the fund the sum of twelve pounds.

18.—That no new member receive any benefit from the fund until his cow has been in the Club one month, and the same rule to apply to every additional cow entered.

19.—That no member shall receive any benefit from the Club whose cow exceeds fourteen years of age.

20.—That a member losing his cow, and making a claim upon the Club for the same, shall be entitled to the skin, but if anything can be made of the carcase the money arising therefrom shall be paid to the use of the members' fund.

21.—That a farrier be appointed by the members of the Club, and that a person be appointed in each district to keep a supply of drinks for the use of the Club.

22.—That should any dispute arise as to the interpretation or application of these rules, the same shall be settled by the Committee, whose decision shall be final.

A List of Members of the Association who have signified their willingness to afford facilities for the extension of the system to the agricultural labourers employed on their estates, and have taken or will take steps to meet such demand for allotments as may exist there, with particulars of the practice on the several properties.

Name	County	Acreage of Estates	Size of the Allotments	Rent as compared with land of equal value let in farms	Remarks
Duke of Richmond and Gordon	Sussex	19,498	17½ perches.	Not higher.	Nearly all cottages have gardens of 13 to 20 rods included in the rent (average, 3*l*. 3*s*. 7*d*.). Is willing to extend the system to all labourers on the estate where circumstances admit.
Duke of Beaufort	Monmouth Gloucester Brecon Glamorgan Wilts	27,299 16,610 4,019 1,218 1,939	All sizes.	In Gloucestershire higher by amount of outgoings: in Monmouth the same	Allotments existed in the present Duke's grandfather's time in 1835, and probably much earlier. They were then called 'poor's plots.' About one-third are not taken. In one village with plots at each end, one plot was unlet so many years that it was thrown into the farm.
Duke of Manchester	Hunts Cambs Bedford	14,774 707 55	30 poles.	Slightly higher. Landlord pays rates and taxes	480 allotments in 6 parishes and 166 cottages with gardens of ½ acre and under.
Duke of Wellington	Hants Herts Somerset Berks	15,847 2,246 529 494	30 poles	Not higher	

				About present farming value	Is prepared to promote the letting of land in suitable quantities to labourers, and is negotiating with tenants for surrender of land for allotments.
Duke of Buckingham and Chandos	Bucks . / Cornwall .	9,511 / 498	1 rood 21 Poles	.	
Duke of Westminster	Cheshire. / Flint . / Denbigh. / Bucks .	15,138 / 3,621 / 744 / 246	¼ to ½ acre .	Not higher.	Tenants without allotments . 257 } 354 / Tenants with allotments . 97 / Tenant cowkeepers . 182 } 354 / Tenants without cows 172 / Tenants without cows or allotments. 130 } 354 / Tenants with one or other . 224 / Summary of holdings under 1 acre . . 236
Marquis of Winchester	Hants	4,796	20 perches .	33s. 6d. to 40s. Tithes and rates free	The allotment lands are situate in the centre of the village.
Marquis of Lansdowne *	Wilts .	11,145	10 perches to 3 acres	In villages about equal; near towns rather lower	Have existed for many years.
Marquis of Exeter	Northampton. / Leicester / Lincoln . / Rutland.	15,384 / 533 / 3,257 / 9,794	From 1 rood to 5 acres. Majority about 1 rood	In some instances higher, but not generally	
	Carried forward	179,902			

* Absent abroad, but Agent believes he can answer for him.

A List of Members of the Association—continued.

Name	County	Acreage of Estates	Size of the Allotments	Rent as compared with land of equal value let in farms	Remarks
Marquis of Bristol	Brought forwrd Suffolk . Lincoln . Essex . Sussex .	179,902 16,953 13,732 11,131 157			Circular has been issued offering allotments to persons not necessarily working on farms of the estate, but resident in parishes where there is property.
Earl of Pembroke .	Wilts . Westmoreland	42,244 31	¼ to ½ acre .	Not usually higher	About 900 on this estate. The custom is a general one in the neighbourhood, but is believed to be capable of considerable increase.
Earl of Devon .	Devon .	20,049	Rather under ¼ acre	The same .	398 allotments now in occupation; more would be provided if required and applied for.
Earl of Suffolk .	Wilts .	11,098	Usually ⅛ acre, but some less	Higher .	Material given to build sheds for small holders if required.
Earl of Denbigh .	Flint .	370 2,848	Trifle under 1 acre	Higher; about to adjust it	Rent has been higher than adjoining land let in farms, but has now been reduced.
Earl of Essex .	Herts . Essex . Warwick .	5,545 3,090 690	10 to 20 poles	Higher .	The Hon. R. Capel hired from a tenant of Lord Essex 6 acres of land to let in allotments.
Earl Poulett .	Somerset . Hants .	10,000 6	20 perches .	Higher, free of rates and tithe	

Name	County		Size of allotment	Rent	Remarks
Earl Cowper.	Herts Notts Derby Kent Northampton. Yorks, W. R. Beds Leicester	10,122 5,294 2,787 2,078 1,064 200 217 17	1 rood. Intends to increase the size	Higher by the amount of outgoings	In Devon a number of small holdings. Is laying out a field in allotments:
Earl Stanhope	Kent Devon	4,343 5,186	15 perches	Rather under	No objection to let land near the villages in allotments at the same rate.
Earl of Buckinghamshire	Derby Bucks	2,583 3,113	1 to 6 acres	The same, but really less, because landlord pays outgoings on allotments	
Earl Bathurst	Gloucester Derby	10,320 3,343	27 perches	In a few cases higher, but not in the majority. Landlord pays all outgoings	In Gloucestershire these allotments have mostly been in existence fifty years.
Earl of Clarendon	Warwick Herts	2,298	⅛ acre.	Higher	
Earl Fortescue	Devon Lincoln Gloucester Cornwall	20,171 5,116 1,071 572	About ¼ acre	If anything, lower in all; in some decidedly lower	Is disposed to afford facilities for the extension of the allotment system.
Earl of Malmesbury	Hants Wilts Dorset	4,155 1,079 212	½ to 20 acres	Much lower, some quit rents	Forty new houses recently built, with ¾ acre each. 120 potato-ground allotments.
		Carried forward 403,187			

A List of Members of the Association—continued.

Name	County	Acreage of Estates	Size of the Allotments	Rent as compared with land of equal value let in farms	Remarks
	Brought forwrd	403,187			
Earl of Cork and Orrery	Somerset	3,398	15 perches	Double	Rental of cottage with garden, 3l. to 4l. per annum.
Earl of Darnley	Kent	9,280	About 22 perches	Higher	All cottages have good gardens, allotments being little sought after.
Earl of Egmont	Sussex	14,021	35 rods	Not higher.	370 allotments on the Sussex estate.
	Surrey	3,466			
	Bucks	585			
	Lincoln	134			
Earl of Carysfort	Hunts	3,972	1 rood.	10s. or 11s. per acre higher	
	Northampton	2,270			
Earl of Onslow	Surrey	11,761	¼ acre.	Slightly higher.	Land on offer in every parish where any is in hand.
	Essex	1,510			
Earl of Romney	Kent	4,023	½ acre.	Not higher	Most of the cottages have good gardens.
	Norfolk	900			
	Kent	5,227	About 1 acre	—	
Earl Nelson	Wilts	7,196	—	Higher, because landlord pays rates and tithe	Most anxious to offer allotments, or to encourage co-operative farming; *vide* article in 'Nineteenth Century,' December 1885.
Earl of Normanton	Wilts	10,069	¼ to ½ acre.	Higher, landlord paying rates and taxes	More allotments on offer than tenants. Average size of gardens, 0a. 1r. 38p.; 136 holdings under 1 acre, and 103 under 50 acres.
	Hants	11,168			
	Northampton	1,065			
	Dorset	1,153			

Member	County	Acreage	Size of allotments	Rent compared	Remarks
Earl Cathcart	Notts	26,771	⅛ to ¼ acre Cow-gaits 2 acres	Not appreciably	Offers have been made for allotments, and wherever required they will be granted.
	Lincoln	5,010			
	Derby	3,729			
	Wilts	1,500			
	Yorks, W.R.	1,026			
	Yorks, N.&W.R.	4,114	20 acres	A trifle higher. Tithe and tax free	In North Riding more small holdings than small tenants. Always give best men cow grass fields. Cottages have good gardens.
	Stafford	1,352			
Earl of Verulam	Herts	8,509	—	Higher	These have been in existence for more than forty years and vary in size; 8 acres in all; three allotments are vacant, and is arranging for allotments over a field of 20 acres.
	Essex	1,492			
Earl St. Germans	Cornwall	5,961	10 to 20 perches. This depends upon the ground attached to cottage	A little higher	Labourers on these estates in Cornwall, Gloucester, and Wiltshire have for many years had allotments.
	Wilts	2,975			
	Gloucester	2,711			
	Kent	1,144			
Earl of Bradford	Salop	10,883	About ¼ acre	About the same	
	Stafford	6,843			
	Warwick	1,906			
	Lancashire	1,958			
	Westmoreland	62			
	Worcester	13			
	Montgomery	15			
	Leicester	6			
	Denbigh	24			
	Carried forward	582,369			

A List of Members of the Association—continued.

Name	County	Acreage of Estates	Size of the Allotments	Rent as compared with land of equal value let in farms	Remarks
	Brought forwrd	582,369			
Earl of Selborne	Hants	1,800	3 acres	Slightly less	Any labourer can have more arable land at once, and pasture as opportunities occur if he wants it.
Viscount Dillon	Oxford	5,444	¼ acre	Not higher, being free of tithe, rates, taxes, &c.	
Dowager Viscountess Downe	Yorks, N.E. & W.R.	22,237	20 perches to 3 acres	Not higher	
Viscount Midleton	Surrey	3,105	—	—	Statement recently issued that allotments would be let slightly over agricultural value, but no applications received. No further demand.
Viscount Barrington	Berks	3,479	10 to 40 perches	44s. 6d. nett; adjoining farm land 45s. 6d. nett per acre	
Viscount Sidmouth	Devon Stafford Berks	4,500 1,000 281	—	—	In Devon all cottagers have large gardens; only one or two requests for land; two labourers rent fields. In Stafford, farmers employ little hired labour; land is let as gardens to miners.

Viscount Combermere	Cheshire Salop Lancashire	9,414 2,447 1,818	—	Only higher where there is a very good house	Allotments are in the centre or close to village
Lord Dacre	Herts Essex Cambs Suffolk	7,170 3,622 2,085 985	About 32 poles	Higher, because landlord pays all rates and taxes	
Lord Zouche	Sussex Stafford	6,654 239	About 30 poles	About the same	
Lord Willoughby de Broke	Warwick Lincoln Northampton Somerset Stafford Anglesea Leicester	12,611 2,930 929 588 555 396 126	From $\frac{1}{4}$ to $1\frac{1}{4}$ acre	The same	Has done a good deal towards the extension of allotments and is disposed to go on with it.
Lord Braye	Leicester	4,000	30 perches	About 20 per cent. higher	No demand for more.
Lord Windsor	Glamorgan Salop Worcester Flint Hereford	17,353 11,204 8,530 317 40	25 perches to 15 acres	Rather higher	Is disposed to increase number of allotments.
Lord Arundell of Wardour	Wilts Cornwall	6,037 182	Nearly 8 acres each	Rather more	In 1878, 428 acres were offered for sale in small lots; 164 acres sold.
Carried forward		724,447			

A List of Members of the Association—continued.

Name	County	Acreage of Estates	Size of the Allotments	Rent as compared with land of equal value let in farms	Remarks
Lord Dormer	Brought forwrd Warwick Bucks	724,447 2,246 1,189	¼ acre	A trifle higher	Two or three of the allotment holders applied for each vacant one till they made up to 7 or 8 acres. Result was heavy loss when bad times came. Discouragement to occupy more than one allotment. Every cottage has, besides, large garden. Three or four labourers have had holdings of 3 to 4 acres each; when young and active they lived very hard lives, and when old sank into extreme poverty.
Lord Herries	Yorks	{ 6,848 2,800	3 or 4 acres	Pasture, 25s. Arable, 20s.	Most cottagers have 3 or 4 acres pasture attached with their cottages. The cows pasture the lanes in summer. Late Lord always wished every married labourer on the estate to be able to keep a cow.
Lord Middleton	Yorks, N.E. and E.R. Notts Leicester Warwick Stafford Derby	14,045 15,015 3,809 3,641 50 16	Arable ¼ to 1 acre; grass 4 acres	Not higher	In some cases the cow allotments are difficult to let. There are exceptions also to the garden allotments being taken up.

Lord Scarsdale	Derby . Leicester	10,437 323	$\frac{1}{8}$ acre.	The same	
Lord Vernon	Derby . Staffordshire	— 7,223	$\frac{1}{4}$ acre.	13s. 6d. each allotment; intended to serve as additional garden	Besides 37 holdings under 35 acres.
Lord Walsingham	Norfolk . Yorks, N. and W.R. Suffolk .	12,126 5,590 1,075	In Yorks, $1\frac{1}{2}$ acre	Not higher.	Has cow-gaits which have been in existence seventy years. Is prepared to let half-acre allotments to labourers at fair agricultural value.
Lord Bagot .	Stafford. Denbigh Merioneth	10,841 18,999 —	30 perches .	Higher, because landlord pays rates and keeps gates and fences	Willing to let land for allotments where required.
Lord Sherborne	Gloucester	15,773	Under acre	Somewhat higher as landlord pays rates &c.	The agricultural parishes which do not possess allotments are in a very small minority. All over the Cotswold there are plenty of allotments, and most landowners have more allotments than they can find tenants for. All cottages have gardens as well.
	Carried forward	856,493			

A List of Members of the Association—continued.

Name	County	Acreage of Estates	Size of the Allotments	Rent as compared with land of equal value let in farms	Remarks
	Brought forwrd	856,493			
Lord Suffield.	Norfolk.	11,828	About 1 acre	Not higher.	System was advocated by father of the present proprietor, who believed there was not an occupier of a labourer's cottage who had not more or less land from which, if thrifty, he could pay his rent
Lord Kenyon.	Flint Denbigh. Lancashire Salop	4,552 3,026 237 126	3 acres	Somewhat higher in proportion	Some allotments cultivated as strawberry gardens and potato plots. 4 cottages with land over 30 acres, 2 ,, ,, 14 ,, 82 ,, ,, 3 ,,
Lord Lyttelton	Worcester	5,907	¼ acre.	Not higher after deducting rates, &c.	
Lord Calthorpe	Warwick Norfolk. Hants Suffolk Stafford Worcester	2,073 2,559 1,390 235 197 16	27 to 40 perches	Not higher when rates, tithes, &c. are deducted	
Lord Henley.	Northampton. Dorset	1,764 3,602	¼ acre.	About the same	Has had forty years' experience of the system, and rarely met with bad cases of cultivation.

Lord Henniker	Suffolk . Norfolk .	10,910 122	¼ acre and upwards	10s. for ¼ acre, free of all out-goings	Practice in existence on this estate over fifty years. One tenant has been in possession fifty-four years. It is found that first-rate men can work an acre or more besides their regular labour. As the men improve in position, more land is let to them.
Lord Rendlesham .	Suffolk .	18,869	¼ to 1 acre .	With title, &c., free, rather higher	Has already instructed agent to receive applications from one to three acres where re-quired. A few men have asked for more land.
Lord Harris .	Kent	4,609	20 perches .	Gardens added to cottages free	Every labourer has been asked if he would like a larger garden. Arrangements have been made to meet the wishes of those few who have ex-pressed such a wish.
Lord Delamere	Cheshire	6,794	—	Not higher .	Chiefly small holdings; labourers also have potato grounds on the farms where they work.
Lord Poltimore Lord Rayleigh	Devon . Essex .	19,883 8,632	30 perches . ½ acre .	Not higher About the same.	Supply of ⅛ to ¼ acre pieces is about equal to demand.
	Carried forward	963,824			

A List of Members of the Association—continued.

Name	County	Acreage of Estates	Size of the Allotments	Rent as compared with land of equal value let in farms	Remarks
Lord Sudeley	Brought forwrd Montgomery . Gloucester . Salop .	963,824 17,158 6,620 175	—	—	The proportion of small farms is fully maintained. There are 76 small holdings under 45 acres, and of those 50 range from 2 to 11 acres. Would be extremely pleased to see no exception to the rule that every labourer has an allotment.
Lord Stanley of Alderley	*	*	$\frac{1}{10}$ acre	The same .	One or two allotments vacant last year. More land has been offered, but has not been applied for. 350 allotments on this estate.
Lord Wenlock	Yorks Salop	15,917 5,227	Allotments, ¼ rood cowgaits and holdings, 10 to 200 acres	The same .	An arable field offered to the inhabitants of one village, but not received a single application.
Lord Egerton of Tatton	Cheshire Lancashire Derby . Durham .	†8,876 †1,870 424 339	$\frac{1}{16}$ of an acre in 10-acre field near Knutsford	Proportionately higher, but same price as accommodation land near a town	Has offered to increase gardens to any reasonable extent, but no applications. There are 63 holdings under 20 acres, 69 over 100 acres, and 14 between 50 and 60 acres.

	County	Acreage	Size of plot	Rather higher; landlord pay rates, &c.	Remarks
Lord Lyveden	Northampton	4,138	20 poles 1 acre	Rather higher; landlord pay rates, &c.	
Lord Fitzhardinge	Gloucester	24,000	About ¼ acre	No rates or taxes charged	
	Dorset	1,476			
	Middlesex	539			
Lord Alington	Dorset	14,756	¼ acre	Not higher	Average rent of allotments on the estate, 1l. 12s. per acre; has rented a field close to Dorchester at 80l., amounting, without outgoings, to 83l. 16s. 4d. It is divided into 144 allotments of ⅓ acre, producing a rental of 47l. 14s.
	Devon	2,587			
	Hants	81			
	Cambs	42			
	Herts	34			
Lord Tollemache of Helmingham	Cheshire	28,651	3 acres	The same	
	Suffolk	7,010			
	Denbigh	35			
	Flint	30			
Lord Norton	Warwick	2,814	¼ acre	Average 30s. an acre	Every able-bodied cottager has ¼ acre, besides garden. System of increasing area of holdings as sufficient capital is saved, up to 10 or 14 acres of pasture for grazing, the man continuing labour; and, if capital enough further saved to leave off labour, 40 to 50 acre small farms.
	Stafford	1,352			
	Rutland	349			
Carried forward		1,109,374			

* Acreage of estate not supplied.   † These figures are understated.

A List of Members of the Association—continued.

Name	County	Acreage of Estates	Size of the Allotments	Rent as compared with land of equal value let in farms	Remarks
	Brought forwrd	1,109,374			
Lord Mount Temple	Hants . . Yorks . . Herts .	6,135 1,249 23	¼ acre. .	With few exceptions, below rent of farms	126 allotments on this estate; 118 cottage gardens. The latter rent free.
Lord Brabourne .	Kent . .	About 5,000 acres	Cottage tenants 30 to 40 perches; allotments average 5 acres	Average 32s. 6d., slightly above average farm rents	At this instant a field of 15 acres thrown on hands within half a mile of a village; made known that it would be let for allotments, but received no applications. Probably the reason was that there was a valuation of 62l. to pay to the outgoing tenant; this the landlord paid, and when a crop of oats has been taken and the field laid down in grass, it will be offered again for allotments.
Lord Northbourne .	Northumberld. Kent . . Durham . .	3,968 3,000 650	About ¼ acre	—	Allotments are near Gateshead; land adjoining is being built on, which prevents extension of system.
Lord Rothschild .	Bucks . . Herts . . Northampton . Middlesex .	5,625 3,959 1,772 620	⅛ to ¼ acre .	Rent lower .	1,500 on this estate. Rent lower than that of adjoining farms.

Name	County	Acreage	Size of allotment	Garden higher, lower		Remarks
Lord St. Oswald	Lincoln, Yorks, W.R.	6,800 2,760	$\frac{1}{2}$ to 1 acre garden, $3\frac{1}{2}$ acres grass	Garden higher, lower	trifle grass	The gardens can only be worked by a plough, which is sometimes done by the farmer for whom the labourer works. Usually worked half in white and half in green crops. Disposed to let $\frac{1}{2}$ acre of land with every new cottage built for agricultural labourer.
Lady Brooke	Essex, Leicester, Northampton, Cambs, Middlesex	8,617 4,411 802 8 6	25 rods	Not higher	.	For the past five years supply has been in excess of demand, and a certain part has had to be laid to the adjoining farms, as labourer would not take more than $\frac{1}{8}$ to $\frac{1}{4}$ of an acre.
Right Hon. Edward Stanhope, M.P.	Lincoln	7,847	$\frac{1}{2}$ to 16 acres	Not higher	.	3s. a week charged for pasturage of cows on a pasture provided for that purpose. Will give an allotment to any man on the estate who desires it.
Right Hon. Sir Massey Lopes, M.P.	Devon, Wilts	11,977 126	From $\frac{1}{8}$ to $\frac{1}{4}$ acre; in some cases considerably more	Not higher	.	Prepared to offer further facilities.
		Carried forward 1,184,729				

A List of Members of the Association—continued.

Name	County	Acreage of Estates	Size of the Allotments	Rent as compared with land of equal value let in farms	Remarks
	Brought forwrd	1,184,729			
Right Hon. George Cubitt, M.P.	Surrey . . Sussex . .	3,989 600	—	About the same	Endeavouring to ascertain and to meet any demand there may be in the villages near where the estates are situate. 10 acres let in allotment in 80 plots, managed by a committee of tradesmen, as garden ground for inhabitants of neighbouring towns.
Right Hon. Henry Chaplin, M.P.	Lincoln .	22,680	1 rood .	Agricultural value only is charged	Most of the cottages on this estate have a good garden in addition attached to the premises.
Right Hon. Edward Heneage, M.P.	Lincoln .	10,761	5 to 10 acres	The same, except near Grimsby; there rent higher	Considers no well-managed estate should be without holdings of all sizes in every village.
The Right Hon. Sir Harry Verney, Bart.	Hants . . Derby . . Bucks . . Anglesea .	650 1,140 6,890 5,078	Garden allotments to 20 poles. Field allotments up to 50	About the same after deduction of tithe and taxes	
Hon. W. C. Carpenter	Yorks .	4,186	Arable ⅛ acre, grass 3 acres	Not at present .	Anxious to afford facilities.

Hon. M. E. G. Finch-Hatton, M.P.	Lincoln . . Notts . .	3,710 741	1 rood arable, 5 to 20 acres grass	Not higher	Desires to see a closer connection with the labourer and the soil. On this estate the plan is an allotment of as much land as he can work in his spare time, and as much grass land as he has money to stock, both at a fair rent. In 1790 more than 80 allotments existed on ancestor's estate in Rutland.
Hon. E. S. Parker-Jervis	Stafford . Warwick .	8,020 164	3 to 7 acres	About 5s. to 10s. more	Wages are high, and labourers do not care to have large allotments.
Hon. Mark Rolle .	Devon .	55,595	⅛ acre	Not higher	For many years past, 22 allotment fields, varying from 1 to 22 acres, making up an aggregate of 1,000 acres, let to 1,000 tenants. Desires to extend the system, especially in the neighbourhood of towns.
Hon. Mrs. Gilbert .	Cornwall .	2,895	—	—	The whole of the estate is let in small holdings to miners.
Sir Herewald Wake, Bart. . Sir G. Osborne, Bart.	Northampton Essex . . Beds . .	1,629 1,512 3,117	¼ acre . 20 poles to 8 acres	Not higher Slightly higher	Altogether 53 acres let in allotments; allows labourers an hour from their work daily to cultivate allotments.
Sir J. R. Blois, Bart.	Suffolk .	6,057	Less than ¼ acre	About the same	Prepared to cut up a field close to the road for allotments if there were any applications.
	Carried forward	1,324,143			

A List of Members of the Association—continued.

Name	County	Acreage of Estates	Size of the Allotments	Rent as compared with land of equal value let in farms	Remarks
	Brought forwrd	1,324,143			
Sir Baldwyn Leighton, Bart.	Shropshire .	4,085	Gardens ¼ to ⅜ acre. Cowland, 2 to 8 acres	About the same; the rents vary	
	Montgomery .	11			
Sir R. W. Proctor-Beauchamp, Bart.	Norfolk .	6,768	From ¼ acre up	About the same	Pasture field recently divided into four 5-acre plots, and notice given that they will be let at the same rent as farmers give. Only two applications. If any demand, is willing to grant any quantity.
	Essex .	378			
Sir A. S. Gooch, Bart.	Suffolk .	7,186	¼ acre .	Not higher	
Sir R. Sheffield, Bart.	Lincoln	9,370	½ to 29 acres	Higher	
Sir R. F. Sutton, Bart.	Lincoln .	4,896	20 poles .	Slightly higher .	Every labourer can have an allotment if he desires. In fact, every man employed has one unless his garden is large enough.
	Notts .	694			
	Berks .	3,756			
Sir G. Wombwell, Bart.	Yorks, N.R. .	12,226	3 acres .	The same .	There are cow clubs on this estate, and every cottage has its own land with cow-house and piggery, besides garden attached to cottage.

Name	County	Acreage	Size	Rent	Remarks
Sir Rainald Knightly, Bart., M.P.	Northampton	8,041	¼ acre	About the same	
Sir W. E. Welby-Gregory, Bart.	Lincoln Leicester Notts	12,292 1,953 2,659	Majority 1 rood	The same	Facilities have been offered on this estate for the last 40 or 50 years.
Sir F. Barrett-Lennard, Bart.	Essex Suffolk	3,691 570	15 rods	Not higher	At Michaelmas, 1885, 24 additional allotments of 20 rods each were let, besides 25 acres in small holdings near village.
Sir Wm. de Capell Brooke, Bart.	Northampton Rutland Leicester	2,966 533 61	10 poles to 10 acres	20 per cent. higher, but landlord pays taxes, rates, repairs roads, fences, &c.	
Sir Alexander Acland-Hood, Bart.	Somerset	11,337	40 perches	About the same	Informed cottagers some years ago, if they would provide themselves with cows, he would provide accommodation. Only one has a cow.
Sir H. J. S. Halford, Bart.	Leicester	3,053	½ rood generally	The same	Offer been made to any amount to labourers living near and willing to take it. Nearly every parish has allotments, and many are vacant. They appreciate them when corn is dear, but not now. 26½ acres have been let for allotments for the last 40 years.
Carried forward		1,420,669			

A List of Members of the Association—continued.

Name	County	Acreage of Estates	Size of the Allotments	Rent as compared with land of equal value let in farms	Remarks
	Brought forwrd	1,420,669			
Admiral Sir G. N. Broke-Middleton, Bart.	Suffolk .	9,500	¼ to ½ acre .		Some years ago offered to lay out 9 acres of land close to village of Coddenham, in allotments at very reasonable rent, but no application. Most anxious to extend system of allotments to agricultural labourers.
Rev. Sir G. C. Shiffner, Bart.	Sussex . Lancashire	4,004 364	3 acres .	About the same	
Sir Wm. Vavasour, Bart.	Yorks, E. & W.R. Stafford	4,666 3,814	½ and ¾ acre up to 2 acres	The rent is only nominal, and seldom paid	
Sir L. J. Jones, Bart.	Norfolk .	3,627	¼ acre .	About the same	Allotments are sublet, which is objectionable.
Rev. Sir C. Clark, Bart.	Suffolk .	3,071	—	—	
Sir J. Neeld, Bart.	Wilts . Middlesex . Herts . Gloucester .	13,112 668 27 5	¼ to 1 acre .	Rather under .	For over 50 years a field has been devoted in each parish for allotments in the proportion of ¼ acre to each family.
Sir J. H. G. Smyth, Bart.	Somerset . Gloucester .	13,542 1,432	31 perches .	Higher .	On estate recently purchased rent of allotments is being reduced, and careful inquiries being made as to sufficiency of allotments.

Sir John Walrond, Bart.	Devon	3,645	Were ¼ acre	Was not higher	Gave allotments several years ago, which were neglected and ultimately given up, partly because better gardens were attached to the cottages. Is still willing to grant allotments. More than 40 years ago obtained land from his father, which he let out in allotments at agricultural value.
Sir P. J. W. Miles, Bart.	Somerset	4,929	¼ acre.	Rather dearer	
Col. Sir Walter B. Barttelot, C.B., M.P.	Sussex	3,633	½ acre.	The same	The cottage gardens average 30 poles. In adjoining parish allotments are being drained and well cultivated with the view to future letting.
Sir W. Marriott, Bart.	Dorset	3,893	30 or 40 perches	Higher for best land	Some of this land, within ½ mile of Blandford, a town of 4,000 inhabitants, is let at 2l. an acre.
Sir H. Foley Vernon, Bart.	Worcester	7,447	¼ acre to 2 acres	Smaller allotments higher. Larger about same	Supplies fruit-trees to tenants.
Sir J. H. Johnson, Kt.	Essex	3,940	—	—	Any amount of land can be had for allotments on application. The number of allotments slightly exceeds the demand.
A. Akers Douglas, Esq., M.P.	Kent	3,753	¼ acre plots	5s. per plot. The rent is about half the letting value of adjoining farms. Landlord pays rates, &c.	
		Carried forward 1,509,741			

A List of Members of the Association—continued.

Name	County	Acreage of Estates	Size of the Allotments	Rent as compared with land of equal value let in farms	Remarks
	Brought forward	1,509,741			
W. W. B. Beach, Esq., M.P.	Hants	6,156	From ⅛ acre to 8 acres	Not higher	
H. R. Farquharson, Esq., M.P.	Wilts . Dorset	895 5,476	¼ acre .	Lower .	Is daily soliciting applications and affording facilities for the extension of the system.
Robert T. Gurdon, Esq., M.P.	Norfolk . Suffolk . N'thumberland	5,027 1,510 4,971	¼ to ½ acre .	Generally lower	The cottagers generally have all had the offer of allotments.
W. G. Mount, Esq., M.P.	Berks . Hants .	4,191 6	40 poles .	Yes; because free of all rates and tithes	
E. W. Harcourt, Esq., M.P.	Middlesex . Oxon . Berks . Sussex .	2 7,520 681 3	—	The same .	Is prepared to rent land to sub-let to tenants of all cottages.
Walter H. Long, Esq., M.P.	Wilts . Somerset Merioneth Montgomery	13,829 841 688 46	¼ acre .	Practically not higher, as landlord pays rates, &c.	
R. H. Paget, Esq., M.P.	Somerset . Stafford .	3,443 134	⅛ to ¼ acre .	Not higher	
J. Round, Esq., M.P.	Essex . Middlesex	5,266 152	⅛ to ¼ acre .	Rent higher	The allotments near Colchester are let at higher rent. Applications having been received for 16 allotments, another field is being set out.

Name	County				Remarks
J. H. Arkwright, Esq.	Hereford	10,559	½ acre (formerly)	20s. per acre	Allotments have been done away with, there being no demand. Ten years ago 190 tenants were asked if they wanted more garden or land; only six replied that they would like an orchard. The question will be repeated early in February.
W. R. Bankes, Esq.	Dorset	19,228	20 perches	3l. per acre after deducting outgoings	Has solicited applications both in practice and by publications.
Rev. Preb. Barnes	Devon	—	6 acres	Rent same	
J. Bateman, Esq.	Essex	1,413	About ¾ acre	Same; landlord pays rates, tithes, &c.	Deposit required from tenant at the rate of 6l. per acre. Returned in full in case of disturbance, and fine of 6l. for such disturbance payable by landlord. When holding given up at tenant's option, deposit returned in full if a certificate is produced from two tenant farmers that plot is in good condition; otherwise it is wholly or partly spent in manure.
G. Bence-Lambert, Esq.	Suffolk	2,625	¼ acre	About the same	
	Yorks, W. R.	717			
	Lancashire	412			
	Cheshire	168			
	Norfolk	7			
	Carried forward	1,605,707			

A List of Members of the Association—continued.

Name	County	Acreage of Estates	Size of the Allotments	Rent as compared with land of equal value let in farms	Remarks
	Brought forwrd	1,605,707			
R. Berkeley, Esq. R. C. L. Bevan, Esq.	Worcester Wilts Berks Middlesex Herts Hants	4,811 2,227 956 469 47 214	¼ and ½ acre ⅓ acre	A little higher Not higher	Property has for many generations been managed as far as possible on the system of small holdings, and allotments were added 40 years ago.
Mrs. Boucherett	Lincoln	5,834	½ acre	Not higher	There remains still in the ' poor's ground ' several allotments unoccupied, and which have been unoccupied for several years.
A. Boughton-Leigh, Esq.	Warwick Northampton	3,100 1,300	—	40s. to 51s. 6d. per acre	Has found it necessary in recent years to reduce the number and average size, so that, solely in consequence of the tenants' diminished needs, the acreage has been reduced by nearly one-half. No fault has ever been found with the position or character of the allotments.
Frederick Bower, Esq.	Sussex	8,500	From about ¼ acre each to ⅓ acre	Lower	

Frank Bradshaw, Esq.	Devon . . Herts . . Somerset . Hants . . Sussex .	6,642 811 396 270 3	15 yards .	Not higher after deducting outgoings	150 acres surrounding the village let to a large number of tenants.
Albert Brassey, Esq.	Oxon . .	4,275	¼ acre .	Rent included in cottage	Has never had applications for allotments. Quite willing to afford facilities for letting land in convenient situations to labourers.
W. E. Brymer, Esq.	Dorset . Somerset .	4,831 415	16½ acres .	2l. and 4l. per acre	Gives prizes for the allotments, which amount to more than the rent received.
Colonel W. E. G. Bulwer	Norfolk . . Kent . .	8,943 108	¼ acre to 4 acres	Not higher .	Has offered 40 acres in one parish alone without any response at present.
R. Carr-Ellison, Esq.	N'thumberland . Durham . .	8,176 1,959	⅛ acre .	Not higher	
Tankerville Chamberlayne, Esq.	Hants . . Leicester . Oxon .	11,000 1,350 13	—	—	Is cutting up land near Southampton for this purpose.
Col. C. M. Chester	Bucks . .	3,129	¾ acre .	Higher, being in village	
J. Talbot Clifton, Esq.	Lancashire .	17,000	Under 1 acre to 10 acres	Higher, except the cottagers' cow pastures, which are as low, or lower than, farms	Recently broken up a farm, and let it field by field to labourers and cow-keepers.
	Carried forward	1,702,486			

A List of Members of the Association—continued.

Name	County	Acreage of Estates	Size of the Allotments	Rent as compared with land of equal value let in farms	Remarks.
		Brought forwrd 1,702,486			
H. R. Corbet, Esq.	Salop, Cheshire	8,856, 127	Various	The same	On this estate, 24 farms of 100 acres and upwards; 18 of 15 to 100 acres; 38 of 3 to 15 acres; 29 of 1 acre to 3 acres. Applications solicited in November 1885. No application from agricultural labourer.
A. Coryton, Esq.	Cornwall, Devon	8,535, 800	20 perches to 2 acres	Not higher	
G. C. Courthorpe, Esq.	Sussex, Kent	3,026, 630	About 20 rods	Rather higher	135 allotments on this estate.
J. S. Crawley, Esq.	Beds, Herts	8,305, 50	In N. Beds 90 poles, in S. Beds 23 poles	—	—
N. C. Curzon, Esq.	Leicester, Derby, Stafford	5,800, 544, 365	Allotments, ⅛ to ⅜ acre; cowgaits 3 acres	Not higher	
M. H. Dalison, Esq.	Lincoln, Kent	3,800, 1,562	3 acres and under; in Kent, gardens	—	Agents instructed to make public a desire to let allotments.
Mrs. Dent	Gloucester, Worcester	3,111, 236	1 chain	Higher	

Name	County	Acreage	Size of holdings	Rent	Remarks
J. D. Wingfield Digby, Esq.	Warwick, Worcester, Dorset	8,904 / 182 / 21,230	20 perches; gardens 15 to 80 pchs.	Not higher after allowing for tithes, rates, &c., paid by landlord	12 freehold, let to 520 tenants. Also between 50 and 60 small holders of under 25 acres each. In Warwickshire all cottagers have good gardens.
Rev. Dixon Dixon-Brown	Northumberland	5,000	20¼ chains	5l. an acre, being accommodation land close to a town	Offered to sell cottagers their holdings, but all preferred to continue to rent them.
Edwards, Col.	Salop	1,281	3½ to 13 acres	Slightly higher to cover cost of repair to buildings, and erecting fencing, &c., i.e. 2l. an acre	This estate was described in 'Three Acres and a Cow.' The system is extended to its full limit, no more land being available; if there were labourers not residing on the estate might apply for it.
T. W. Evans, Esq.	Derby, Stafford	6,799 / 1,327	400 to 800 square roods ¼ acre.	Higher	
W. R. G. Farmer, Esq.	Suffolk, Surrey, Cambs, Hunts	2,258 / 1,100 / 827 / 687		30s. acre, about the same rent as the farms	Has a good many allotments in Suffolk and a few in Surrey.
J. J. Farquharson, Esq.	Dorset	6,063	Grass 5 to 20 acres arable, 1 to 8 acres	Same	
Robt. Fellowes, Esq.	Norfolk, Huntingdon	7,758 / 1	¼ acre to 10 acres	Not higher.	Has 146 small holdings, as well as runs for 29 cows or horses at 2l. 2s. per acre per cow or horse.
		Carried forward 1,811,700			

A List of Members of the Association—continued.

Name	County	Acreage of Estates	Size of the Allotments	Rent as compared with land of equal value let in farms	Remarks
	Brought forwrd	1,811,700			
W. O. Foster, Esq.	Salop . Worcester . Stafford .	8,547 1,917 874	—	Gardens generally let with cottages at low rent	One or two allotments have been abandoned and given up.
W. H. Fox, Esq. . Edward Frewen, Esq.	Oxford . Sussex . Leicester . Kent . Rutland .	4,500 3,590 4,300 29 55	¼ acre. Leicester, arable 7 to 60 perches, meadow and pasture 3 acres. Sussex, ¼ acre	Slightly higher . Leicester, higher for very small garden allotments, not for larger ones. Sussex, about 10s. per acre higher	Not all let, some not half-farmed.
C. Davies Gilbert, Esq.	Sussex .	3,526	12 perches to 5 acres .	About equal after rates and taxes are paid by the landlord .	
A. L. Goddard, Esq. . J. Godman, Esq. .	Wilts . Sussex . Surrey .	3,821 2,540 2,460	50 acres . ¼ to 1½ acre	Higher . Not higher.	All farm tenants have liberty to underlet for allotments. All allotments occupied by men not cottage tenants on the estate.
H. D. Greene, Esq., Q.C.	Salop .	Upwards of 4,000	—	None at present	No application has been made for allotments and no demand exists, but is endeavouring to offer them.

Ed. Hammersley, Esq.	Oxon			About equal, viz. 5d. per pole	Demand not equal to the supply.
C. S. Hardy, Esq.	Kent	3,500	97 tenants hold 16 acres 20 perches to 2 acres	The same as nearly as possible	There were a good many 25 years since, which, becoming vacant, and not applied for, were absorbed in larger holdings.
T. Hare, Esq.	Norfolk Devon	11,310 383	¼ acre.	Real rent same as that of the farms after paying taxes, &c.	
W. J. Harris, Esq.	Devon	2,900	3 to 38 acres	Somewhat higher but low rents as to value	Has for last 12 years been engaged in creating small holdings on the property.
Hartley Estates (H. C. Bazett, agent)	Berks Gloucester	4,952 2,772	20 poles to 2 acres	Arable land slightly higher, garden land, 1s. 3d.	Applications already solicited from agricultural labourers, but none received; they find the gardens as much as they can manage.
A. P. Lonsdale Heywood, Esq.	Salop Cheshire	4,448 688	Under 1 acre to 2 acres. Tenements 1 to 300 acres and over	Not higher. Cottage and gardens 3l. to 4l. per annum	
Mrs. Heywood	Salop Lancs	3,364 685	Various 1 to 250 acres ¼ acre.	Not higher.	52 holdings under 10 acres.
E. W. Hollond, Esq.	Suffolk Norfolk Dorset	2,349 1,038 856		Not higher.	20 acres are occupied by 100 tenants.
	Carried forward	1,891,104			

A List of Members of the Association—continued.

Name	County	Acreage of Estates	Size of the Allotments	Rent as compared with land of equal value let in farms	Remarks
	Brought forwrd	1,891,104			
A. D. Hussey-Freke, Esq.	Wilts .	3,911	⅛ to ¼ acre .	Not higher.	Land adjoining town of Highworth at present being let in allotments.
G. M. Hutton, Esq.	Lincoln .	3,431	1 rood. .	Not higher	Any land suitable for allotment would be let if desired to labourers on the estate, or others in the parishes.
Mrs. Honywood .	Essex .	6,898	—	—	
	Kent .	561			
W. H. Iremonger, Esq.	Hants .	5,103	30 poles .	Slightly higher	Allotment ground better land
F. M. E. Jervoise, Esq.	Hants .	6,183	⅛ to ¼ acre .	Not higher.	Where cottage gardens are small, allotments are added rent free.
	Wilts .	3,663			
G. E. Jarvis, Esq.	Lincoln .	2,529	Good garden and 2 roods land	Not considered higher	
	Warwick .	1,230			
	Notts .	958			
	Kent .	3			
	Leicester .	2,468			
Mrs. Keane .	Cheshire.	4,706	3 or 4 acres .	Very little higher, 20s. an acre	
T. Kekewich, Esq.	Cornwall .	2,603	30 perches .	About the same	
	Devon .	2,131			
R. W. Ketton, Esq.	Norfolk .	4,442	¼ acre.	When separate, 10s. more per acre	

Name	County	Acreage	Allotment	Rent	Remarks
Colonel Kingscote, G. C.B.	Gloucester	3,956	¼ acre	About the same, plus outgoings	On this estate there are over 170 tenants occupying ¼ acre to 1 acre, and more allotments than tenants.
Montague Knight, Esq.	Hants	5,044	¼ to ½ acre	Not higher	
Rev. W. C. E. Ky-naston	Salop, Montgomery	3,518 1,200	3 acres	Slightly higher	
Lt. Col. H. B. Lane	Stafford, Berks	2,707	27 to 41 perches	10s. to 20s. per acre higher	There are as many allotments as required.
Mrs. Lawrence	Gloucester	3,447	About 33 perches	5s. per chain, owner paying rates, &c.	
W. Leigh, Esq.	Gloucester	3,847	¼ acre	About the same after deducting tithe, rates, &c.	16 acres let in allotments; each labourer who requires it has ¼ acre.
Thos. Barrett-Lennard, Esq.	Norfolk	2,124	1 acre and upwards	Lower	More allotments would be let if there were any demand, but the land available is poor, and the tendency is to consolidate.
H. L'Estrange, Esq.	Norfolk	7,803	¼ acre	Very slightly higher	
Col. M. Lockwood.	Essex, Glamorgan, Monmouth	2,300 1,226 1,440	20 poles	Generally much under	
Col. W. B. Long	Suffolk, Cambs	2,850 784	20 to 80 roods	Not higher	
	Carried forward	1,984,170			

A List of Members of the Association—continued.

Name	County	Acreage of Estates	Size of the Allotments	Rent as compared with land of equal value let in farms.	Remarks
	Brought forwrd	1,984,170			
G. F. Luttrell, Esq.	Somerset . Devon .	15,374 154	15 perches .	Much lower	Rent is much lower in some cases than on adjoining farms, and in no case higher.
W. Dalziel Mackenzie, Esq.	Oxford . Bucks . Suffolk . Norfolk . Lancs . Berks .	2,216 1,867 8,188 5,737 — 50	¼ to 20 acres	Not higher, in many cases lower	Offered 200 acres close to Henley, but few applications. In Norfolk and Suffolk, about 100 allotments near the town. A field of 19 acres recently laid out for more allotments. Rent 1l. an acre.
L. K. Mainwaring, Esq.	Salop . Cheshire Flint . Denbigh.	3,664 1,755 205 82	6 to 20 acres	Not generally higher	
C. Massingberd-Mundy, Esq.	Lincoln .	3,358	1 rood .	Somewhat higher	
Lt.-Genl. Marshall	Surrey .	700	¼ acre .	Free .	Allotments given free of rent, rates and taxes.
E.P.Monckton,Esq.	Northampton. Rutland .	928 2,183	½ rood to lane	Not much higher but so as to include rates, &c.	
Geo. Moore, Esq.	Derby . Warwick	1,310 272	½ rood.	Not higher	In Warwickshire the allotments were done away with, no one wanting them.

			¼ to 4 acres.	Agricultural gardens and allotments low rent. Artisan allotments, about 3l. to 3l. 10s. per acre after deducting outgoings	Nearly every cottage on the estate has from ¼ to ¾ acre of garden land.
W. More-Molyneux, Esq.	Surrey .	2,500	¼ to 4 acres.		
R. A. Morritt, Esq.	Yorks, N. and W.R.	6,000	More than 8 acres each	Not higher	17 holdings under 10 acres, 7 under 20 acres; 13 of these tenants are in constant work.
W. Wykeham Musgrave, Esq.	Westmoreland Gloucester . Oxford . Bucks . Durham . Kent .	58 4,399 4,426 2,461 1,464 460	20 poles to each person	Higher; 56s. an acre	Allotments and cow lands established 50 years at least. Accommodation land close to Thame town.
John Chaworth Musters, Esq.	Notts .	8,211	⅛ acre .	A little higher, but landlord pays all rates, and keeps fences in repair	
G. Neville, Esq. .	Lincoln .	3,300	½ to 4 acres	Pasture equal. Arable rather higher	
G. Onslow Newton, Esq.	Cambs .	2,794	½ acre .	Rather higher .	Already let 80 acres at farm rates in 1 to 4 acre lots.
G. W. Nicholl, Esq.	Huntingdon . Glamorgan . Monmouth .	3,209 1,375 1,956	Labourers 2 to 6 acres, artisans 6 to 14 acres of pasture	The same	—
	Carried forward	2,074,826			

A List of Members of the Association—continued.

Name	County	Acreage of Estates	Size of the Allotments	Rent as compared with land of equal value let in farms	Remarks
H. G. Palmer, Esq.	Brought forwrd Berks . Oxon .	2,074,826 3,818 1,208			
Philip O. Papillon, Esq.	Sussex . Essex . Kent .	3,736 1,323 17	10 to 20 poles 20 perches .	Higher About double .	The allotments in Essex are 14 acres in extent. Average rent 5s. per annum, including cost of fencing.
James S. Pennyman, Esq.	Yorks, N.R. . Durham .	2,211 960	⅛ acre each; total, 20 acres, all gardens	Not higher	
Mrs. Perry-Herrick	Leicester . Monmouth . Hereford . Radnor .	7,045 4,094 3,041 52	600 square yards	The same .	Certain allotment lands were sold for building sites by adjoining owner two years since. Land on this estate was offered to take its place, but no application received.
Rev. W. Graham F. Piggot	Cambs .	1,400	¼ acre .	Slightly, but landlord pays tithe, rates & taxes	Land let to labourers other than those who work on the estate, and ready to let more if wanted.
General Pitt-Rivers	Dorset . Wilts .	24,942 2,762	60 to 80 perches	About the same .	Between 600 and 700. For many years all labourers who required allotments have had them, in addition to those working on estate. Willing to grant extension provided not too much is let to prevent earning weekly wages.

J. R. Pine-Coffin, Esq.	Devon	3,854	20 yards to ¼ acre	A little higher	
J. C. Mansell-Pleydell, Esq.	Dorset	8,699	3 to 10 acres	The same	
W. F. Plowden, Esq.	Salop, Northants	5,225 735	Labourers ¼ acre; tradesmen, 3 to 10 acres	Not higher to labourers, slightly higher to others	
Melville Portal, Esq.	Hants	10,966	Reduced by general desire from 20 rods to 10 rods each	Not higher; the allotments are let free from tithes, rates & taxes	
H. B. Mackworth-Praed, Esq.	Suffolk	2,198	¼ to ½ acre	Higher; landlord pays rates, &c.	Is going to make further reduction of rent in addition to reduction made last year.
E. R. Pratt, Esq.	Norfolk	3,232	1 to ½ acre	Nett rent about 10 p.c. higher	161 at ¼ acre.
Decie R. Prescott, Esq.	Worcester Hereford Salop	2,169 1,112 6	—	—	Every cottage has garden. Allotments tried, but abandoned; ready to let garden allotments or pasture at 20s. per acre.
F. Rodd, Esq.	Cornwall	7,012	20 yards garden and 20 yards allotment	The same	Allotments were let at from 3d. to 6d. per yard, according to wages of tenants as under or over 12s. a week, but not being taken up the system was abandoned.
	Carried forward	2,177,543			

A List of Members of the Association—continued.

Name	County	Acreage of Estates	Size of the Allotments	Rent as compared with land of equal value let in farms	Remarks
	Brought forwrd	2,177,543			
W. Sandford, Esq.	Somerset . Devon .	5,057	About ¼ acre	About the same, less when let separate from cottage	All cottages have ¼-acre gardens.
J. S. Scott-Chad, Esq.	Norfolk .	5,213	½ to 1 acre .	Nominal rent	
Warden Sergison, Esq.	Sussex .	4,850	¼ acre .	About the same.	Has advertised for applications, but no one will take an allotment beyond those already existing.
R. B. Sheridan, Esq.	Dorset .	11,468	—	The same	
C. C. Sibthorp, Esq.	Lincoln . Herts .	6,000 1,700	½ to 1 rood .	Higher, to cover rates, &c.	
Cecil Smyth-Pigott, Esq.	Somerset	6,000	¼ acre . .	The same as adjoining farms	
W. Stanhope Spencer, Esq.	Yorks, W.R.	11,357	1 rood. Holdings 10 to 40 acres	The same, landlord paying rates and taxes	Has encouraged applications and given prizes. Spade cultivation succeeded by plough, the labourers hiring this work from the farmers.
Thomas Taylor, Esq.	Lancaster Oxford . Bucks .	4 7,185 839	21 poles .	About 10 per cent higher.	

F. Townsend, Esq.	Warwick / Worcester	2,378 / 1,387	⅛ to ½ acre	Higher; proposes to reduce it	Approves of arrangement by which pasture as grazing ground could be let to the labourer or to labourers combining.
C. W. A. Troyte, Esq.	Devon / Somerset	6,627 / 180	20 perches to ¼ acre	Rent free	Every cottage has a good garden.
H. R. Upcher, Esq.	Norfolk / Bedford	1,748 / 945	¼ acre	Not higher	Every labourer on this estate has had an allotment for years.
J. Waddingham, Esq.	Cardigan / Gloucester / Montgomery	10,963 / 1,969 / 402	2 to 6 acres	Not materially higher	In Gloucestershire the glebe is generally let in allotments of from ½ acre upwards.
R. J. Weld, Esq.	Dorset / Hants	15,478 / 47	½ acre average	Not higher after deducting rates &c.	Employers usually give each labourer potato-ground. There are 50 small occupations of mixed land let with cottages, 34 of which contain 1 to 5 acres, the remainder from 5 to 10 acres.
T. Vernon Wentworth, Esq.	Yorks / Suffolk / Northampton / Bucks	5,111 / 3,117 / 672 / 49	6 acres	Higher	No application is refused for garden allotments.
Capt. Whitmore G. C. Douglas	Essex	8,545	20 rods	5s. for 20 rods	Prepared to let as much land for allotment as people will take, but there is no demand.
R. G. Wilberforce, Esq.	Sussex	3,554	40 poles to 1 acre	1l. an acre, the same as let to farmers	
	Carried forward 2,300,388				

K

A List of Members of the Association—continued.

Name	County	Acreage of Estates	Size of the Allotments	Rent as compared with land of equal value let in farms	Remarks
C. Wingfield, Esq.	Brought forwrd Salop	2,300,388 3,574	1 to 20 acres	The same	Estate let in small holdings of from 5 to 20 acres and upwards.
Ed. Wingfield, Esq.	Bedford. Gloucester. Oxford. Glamorgan	1,178 4,333 1,766 6,463	¼ acre.	Not higher, after considering rates and defaulters	No agricultural labourers on Glamorganshire estates.
Thos. Wood, Esq.	Brecon. Yorks, N.R. Middlesex. Surrey. Carmarthen. Cardigan. Oxford. Radnor.	3,796 1,820 1,428 1,071 875 601 305 82	About ¼ acre of garden	Less rent	
W. Woods, Esq.	Hants. Lancashire.	3,649 49	20 rods	Not higher	On own farm, 3,000 acres men have a piece of potato-land gratis.
C.B.E. Wright, Esq.	Yorks, N. and W.R.	5,200	1 rood.	Not higher	Several garden allotments on hand, there being no tenants.
Wm. Wyndham, Esq.	Wilts. Somerset. Devon. Surrey.	5,734 11,231 6,740 3	About 20 perches	Rather higher	Is open to extend the allotment system.
	Total	2,360,286			

It will be seen from the above tables that 248 owners of large estates, amounting in the aggregate to upwards of 2,441,620 acres of land, are prepared to meet the demand for allotments by those residing on their estates. The total area in England and Wales under cultivation is 32,544,000 acres, of which rather over one-fourteenth is owned by those whose estates are referred to above.

The fact must not be lost sight of that these particulars refer, with very few exceptions, only to the estates of owners of 3,000 acres and upwards to whom my queries were addressed, many of whom did not reply to the circular.

If owners of so large a portion of the cultivated area of England have, in response to the inquiries of a private individual, expressed their willingness to afford allotments to the labourers, there can be little doubt that a Government inquiry will reveal a still more satisfactory state of affairs.

NUMBER OF LABOURERS AND ACREAGE OF ESTATES OF MEMBERS IN EACH COUNTY WHERE ALLOTMENTS ARE APPRECIATED.

County	Labourers in each County according to Census of 1881	Acreage of the Estates of Members of the Association in each County.
Bedford.	14,749	15,700
Berks	18,638	21,912
Bucks	13,277	36,747
Carmarthen	3,242	875
Cambridge	20,994	8,680
Cheshire	16,558	75,492
Cornwall	15,393	42,710
Derby	7,672	36,618
Devon	29,282	141,676
Dorset	14,222	143,363
Essex	37,742	73,360
Gloucester	18,650	109,440
Hampshire	24,985	91,880
Hereford	11,123	14,752
Herts	16,877	40,604
Huntingdon	6,782	22,816

LABOURERS AND ACREAGE OF ESTATES—*continued.*

County	Labourers in each County according to the Census of 1881	Acreage of the Estates of Members of the Association in each County
Kent	39,528	34,835
Leicester	12,758	40,669
Lincoln	42,057	108,842
Monmouth	4,784	34,789
Norfolk	3,933	93,113
Northampton	19,407	42,506
Nottingham	13,312	47,132
Oxford	17,084	37,073
Rutland	2,501	2,616
Shropshire . . .	18,159	80,601
Somerset	26,479	86,361
Stafford	15,666	39,536
Suffolk	35,515	107,119
Surrey	13,948	34,612
Sussex	28,654	73,393
Warwick	16,851	53,133
Wilts	21,611	130,953
Worcester	13,620	32,615
York	58,738	127,459

PRINTED BY
SPOTTISWOODE AND CO., NEW-STREET SQUARE
LONDON

Printed in the United States
By Bookmasters